NAVIGATING ADULTHOOD

ESSENTIAL LIFE SKILLS FOR TEENAGE BOYS

A PRACTICAL GUIDE TO THRIVE IN THE MODERN WORLD

JAMES FOSTER

© Copyright 2024 - All rights reserved.

The content contained within this book may not be reproduced, duplicated, or transmitted without direct written permission from the author or the publisher. Under no circumstances will any blame or legal responsibility be held against the publisher, or author, for any damages, reparation, or monetary loss due to the information contained within this book, either directly or indirectly.

Legal Notice:

This book is copyright protected. It is only for personal use. You cannot amend, distribute, sell, use, quote or paraphrase any part, or the content within this book, without the consent of the author or publisher.

Disclaimer Notice:

Please note the information contained within this document is for educational and entertainment purposes only. All effort has been executed to present accurate, up to date, reliable, complete information. No warranties of any kind are declared or implied. Readers acknowledge that the author is not engaged in the rendering of legal, financial, medical or professional advice. The content within this book has been derived from various sources. Please consult a licensed professional before attempting any techniques outlined in this book. By reading this document, the reader agrees that under no circumstances is the author responsible for any losses, direct or indirect, that are incurred as a result of the use of the information contained within this document, including, but not limited to, errors, omissions, or inaccuracies.

TABLE OF CONTENTS

Introduction 11

1. **Emotional Intelligence** 13

    1.1 Navigating Your Emotions: Beyond Anger and Joy 13

        Understanding the Spectrum 14

        Identifying Emotions 14

        Emotional Triggers 17

        Healthy Expression 19

    1.2 The Art of Self-Control: Keeping Cool Under Pressure ... 21

        Recognizing Pressure Points 21

        Breathing and Counting Techniques 23

        Deep Belly Breathing 24

        Pursed Lip Breathing 25

        4-7-8 Breath 25

        Alternate Nostril Breathing 25

        Lion's Breath. 26

        Holotropic Breathwork 26

        Sitali Breath 26

        Humming Bee Breath (Bhramari) 27

        Long-Term Strategies 27

        Learning from Experience 29

    1.3 Empathy: Walking in Someone Else's Shoes 31

        The Basics of Empathy 31

        Empathy vs. Sympathy vs. Compassion 32

    Listening Skills 33

    Perspective-Taking 36

    Empathy in Action 38

    Another Warning 39

  1.4 Building Resilience: Bouncing Back from Setbacks 39

    Understanding Resilience 40

    The Role of Optimism 42

    Learning from Failure 43

  1.5 Self-Reflection: The Key to Personal Growth 44

    The Importance of Self-Reflection 45

    Journaling Techniques 47

    Feedback from Others 48

  1.6 Summary 51

2. **Self-Identity And Confidence** 53

  2.1 Discovering Who You Are: Beyond Labels and Stereotypes 53

    Peeling Back the Layers 53

    Values and Beliefs 54

    Interests and Passions 56

    Overcoming Societal Expectations 57

  2.2 Confidence Building 101: Overcoming Self-Doubt 58

    Identifying Sources of Self-Doubt 58

    Positive Affirmations 59

    Surrounding Yourself with Positivity 61

  2.3 The Power of Positive Self-Talk 61

    Recognizing Negative Self-Talk 62

Changing the Narrative 62

The Role of Self-Compassion 63

Practicing Gratitude 64

2.4 Setting Personal Boundaries: Learning to Say No 65

The Importance of Boundaries 65

Identifying Your Boundaries 66

Communicating Boundaries 67

2.5 Embracing Your Uniqueness: Celebrating Individuality .. 68

What Makes You Unique 68

The Strength in Diversity 69

Overcoming the Fear of Judgment 69

2.6 Summary 71

3. **Making And Maintaining Friendships** 73

3.1 Finding Your Tribe: Making New Friends 73

Opening Up to New Experiences 74

The Role of Extracurricular Activities 75

Online Communities 75

3.2 The Art of Conversation: Beyond Small Talk 76

Mastering Small Talk 77

Active Listening 79

Asking Open-Ended Questions 79

Conversational Etiquette 80

3.3 Dealing with Conflict: Healthy Resolutions 80

Identifying the Source of Conflict 81

Effective Communication Skills 82

Forgiveness and Moving Forward 83

    3.4 Being a Good Friend: Support and Trust 84

        The Pillars of Friendship 84

        Showing Empathy and Support 85

    3.5 Navigating Peer Pressure: Staying True to Yourself 86

        Understanding Peer Pressure 87

        Confidence in Decision-Making 87

        The Power of "No" 88

    3.6 Summary 89

4. **Understanding Family Dynamics 91**

    4.1 Family Roles: Understanding Each Other 91

        The Family System 91

        Individual Needs vs. Family Expectations 94

        Changing Roles Over Time 96

        Contributing to Family Life 97

    4.2 Communicating with Parents and Older Siblings: Bridging the Gap 98

        Understanding Generational Differences 98

        Effective Communication Strategies 101

        Building Mutual Respect 103

        Dealing with Disagreements 105

    4.3 Handling Sibling Rivalry: From Conflict to Cooperation 106

        Root Causes of Sibling Rivalry 106

        Fair Play 107

        Turning Rivalry into Teamwork 108

4.4 Appreciating Family Values: Tradition Meets the Modern World 109

The Importance of Tradition 109

Balancing Tradition and Individuality 110

Modernizing Traditions 111

Creating New Traditions 112

4.5 Creating Your Support System: Beyond Blood Relations 112

Defining "Family" 113

Building a Chosen Family 115

The Importance of Support Networks 116

Maintaining Connections 116

4.6 Summary 117

5. Succeeding In School 119

5.1 Mastering Time Management: Balancing School and Life 119

Prioritization is Key 120

Creating a Schedule 121

Avoiding Procrastination 121

Tools for Time Management 122

5.2 Effective Study Techniques: Beyond Cramming 123

Active Learning Strategies 123

Study or Work Environment 124

Memory Aids 126

The Pomodoro Technique 128

5.3 Coping with Academic Pressure: Stress Management Strategies 129

    Recognizing Stress 129

    Healthy Stress Relief 130

    Seeking Support 130

    Balanced Lifestyle 131

5.4 Setting Academic Goals: Short-Term Wins and Long-Term Visions 131

    SMART Goals 131

    Tracking Progress 134

5.5 Exploring Extracurriculars: Building a Well-Rounded Profile 134

    Benefits of Extracurricular Activities 135

    Finding Your Interests 137

    Balancing Academics and Extracurriculars 138

5.6 Summary 139

6. Career Exploration And Goal Setting 141

6.1 Dream Big: Uncover Your Passions and Talents 141

    Self-Assessment 142

    Exploring Passions 143

    Vision Board Creation 143

    Inspiration from Role Models 144

6.2 Goal Setting: Creating a Roadmap for Success 144

    Long-Term Vision 145

    Actionable Steps 145

    Flexibility in Planning 146

6.3 The World of Work: Understanding Different Careers ... 147

    Career Research 147

  Informational Interviews 148

  Emerging Industries... 151

  Workplace Skills... 152

 6.4 Networking 101: Making Connections that Count 155

  Building a Professional Network.. 155

  The Importance of Mentors 157

  Networking Etiquette... 157

  Leveraging Social Media... 159

 6.5 Preparing for the Future: Skills for Tomorrow's World . 160

  Future-Proofing Your Skills.. 160

  Continuous Learning 161

  Career Adaptability.. 161

  Innovation and Creativity 162

 6.6 Summary 162

References **169**

INTRODUCTION

The contents of this book are for young men between the ages of thirteen and fifteen. At this age, you are realizing that life is starting to look very different from when you were a child, and you're dealing with responsibilities and pressures that younger boys don't need to worry about yet.

Trust me, I get it. Some years ago, I was in your very position. But with similar guidance as I'm going to pass onto you through this book, I was able to grow into (what I like to think of as a) capable man who has lived my life with a thirst for knowledge, an openness to learning new lessons, and an all-around zest for life.

Through this book, I hope to guide you through several areas that I deem to be important in this stage of your life, including (but not limited to) emotional intelligence, self-identity and confidence, the importance in making and maintaining friendships, understanding family dynamics (and especially how they will change as you get older), succeeding in school, career exploration, financial literacy, general life management of a young adult, the ever-changing digital world, physical health, and navigation of mental and emotional well-being.

Now, before you close this book and think it's just like any other "self-help" book, please stick with me. I carefully planned and wrote this to help you, and I've even sprinkled in several stories and personal examples from my own life for you to relate to. You see, I don't want you to read these words and think that I am trying to "preach" to you. On the contrary, I'm actually trying to help you save yourself a lot of time and effort that I've seen other young men waste on their journeys to becoming the best possible versions of themselves.

Alright... thanks for making it this far. ☺ That shows great promise and character on your part.

Now, let's dive into your journey of empowerment and growth as a young man.

Waste no more time arguing about what a good man should be. Be one.

~Marcus Aurelius

CHAPTER ONE:
EMOTIONAL INTELLIGENCE

1.1 NAVIGATING YOUR EMOTIONS: BEYOND ANGER AND JOY

One of the most important lessons you need to learn as you transition into manhood is how to manage and regulate your emotions. You can no longer fly off the cuff and have temper tantrums and, on the other end of the spectrum, it's not always appropriate to indulge in self-celebration for menial tasks (like when making a basket at the park or finishing your vegetables at dinner).

Such ups and downs in emotional expression may be fine for younger children, but you are no longer one of them. You're a young man, and your life will be easier if you learn how to act like it.

Understanding the Spectrum

I've already touched on this, but it bears repeating and some further inspection. In order to identify your emotions, you have to understand the vast range that most humans have. This knowledge is referred to as emotional intelligence.

According to Lisa Feldman Barrett, a modern emotions theorist, emotions are constructed by the brain in response to sensory, input, past experiences, and cultural context. So, emotions aren't simply reactions to external events. Instead, they are shaped by our internal processing and interpretation of such events.

However, emotions are also believed to develop from a neutral baseline. So, something like walking around in a mall without feeling particularly happy or sad can turn into positive feelings based on positive events—like finding a shirt that you've been wanting forever in your size and on sale—or negative based on negative events—like finding that same shirt but instead only in a size too big or too small.

Identifying Emotions

Even if we understand that we're having a positive or negative emotion, it isn't always the easiest to decipher what that feeling actually is. For example, say you're walking down the street, you hear a dog barking, and it startles you. The next question you have to ask is why—are you afraid, excited, or somewhere in between?

Here's a chart that might help you navigate your emotions (and don't worry, people of every age sometimes need help with this):

Broad Feeling (Layer 1) / Deeper Feelings (Layer 2) / Even Deeper Feelings (Layer 3)		
Anger	Enraged	Hateful
		Hostile
	Exasperated	Agitated
		Frustrated
	Irritable	Annoyed
		Aggravated
	Jealous	Envious
		Resentful
	Disgusted	Contemptuous*
		Revolted
Sadness	Hurt	Agonized
		Disturbed
	Unhappy	Miserable
		Disheartened
	Disappointed	Dismayed
		Displeased
	Shameful	Regretful
		Guilty
	Lonely	Isolated
		Neglected
	Gloomy	Hopeless
		Depressed
Surprise	Stunned	Shocked
		Bewildered
	Confused	Disillusioned
		Perplexed
	Amazed	Awe-struck

Joy	Overcome	Astonished
		Speechless
		Astounded
	Moved	Touched
		Stimulated
	Peaceful	Serene
		Tranquil
	Content	Pleased
		Satisfied
	Happy	Delighted
		Jovial
	Cheerful	Playful
		Amused
	Proud	Triumphant
		Illustrious**
	Optimistic	Hopeful
		Eager
	Excited	Enthusiastic
		Zealous
	Euphoric	Elated
		Jubilant***
Love	Enchanted	Enthralled
		Rapturous****
	Romantic	Enamored
		Passionate
	Affectionate	Compassionate
		Warmhearted
	Sentimental	Nostalgic
		Tender
	Grateful	Appreciative
		Thankful
Fear	Scared	Frightened
		Helpless
	Terrified	Panicked
		Hysterical
	Insecure	Inferior

		Inadequate
	Nervous	Worried
		Anxious
	Horrified	Mortified
		Dreadful

Please keep in mind that all of these feelings can blend and bleed into one another. For instance, anger and sadness can go hand-in-hand while jealousy, disgust, hurt, and unhappiness can too.

What's important is the ability to recognize the base (or bases) of our feelings and then dig deeper to find out what's really going on inside of us. That's what an emotionally intelligent person is able to do.

*   showing or expressing contempt or disdain; scornful; disrespectful.

**   well known, respected, and admired for past achievements.

***   feeling or expressing great happiness and triumph.

****   characterized by, feeling, or expressing great pleasure or enthusiasm.

Emotional Triggers

Once you have a better understanding of your emotions, you should also try to recognize what triggers—including anything like memories, experiences, or events—that spark intense, negative emotional reactions in you.

Common situations that trigger emotions can include rejection, betrayal, unjust treatment, challenged beliefs, feeling helplessness, being excluded or ignored, disapproval or criticism, feeling unwanted or smothered, insecurity, and loss of independence.

If you need a little help identifying triggers, make sure that you are really taking time out of your day to listen to your body. Responses like a pounding heart, upset stomach, shakiness or dizziness, and sweaty palms can sometimes indicate to you when you're having a negative reaction to something going on around you.

Then, once you notice any of the signs above, try to take a step back and consider what just happened to you to activate such emotions. Say for instance, you worked really hard to get a grade up in a class you tend to struggle in. But when your parents saw your report card, they didn't say anything about it. Understandably, that could lead you to feel angry, sad, and/or frustrated. In that case, the perceived failure of your parents to acknowledge your hard work is a trigger for you.

However, the digging still isn't done there. Instead, you should continue to think back to another time when you felt the exact same way. Was it when you tried your best and beat your previous years' time to run a mile, and your gym teacher didn't say anything? Or maybe when you went out of your way to wash your parents or guardian's car, and they didn't even notice or acknowledge your work?

Regardless of the trigger, after finding the cause and root of it, you will probably want to ask yourself what the best way to handle the situation now and in future will be. Perhaps, in the grades example, you may feel it's best to express your frustration to your parents. But please try to be as open and honest as possible. Coming out of the gates accusatory likely won't get you anywhere—and your parents will automatically go on the defense. But instead opening the conversation by saying something like, "Hey, did you notice I got my grade up?" is a much better approach.

But please also consider the possibility that you need to be prouder of yourself. That's also part of being a young adult. Sometimes you have to celebrate your own quiet victories, and that has to be enough. For example, once you get a job, it's unlikely that someone is going to congratulate you at the end of every day for putting in your shift. No. That's your job, and that's what you're supposed (and getting paid) to do. So, at the end of the day, you may need to settle for knowing you did a job well done and just go home for the night.

Healthy Expression

Whether we like it or not, our bodies are hard-wired to feel emotions. But whether we choose to express them or not is up to us.

And that decision will depend on the particular emotion, the setting you're in, and the people who are around you at the time.

Let's consider you are out to dinner with family or friends, and a server brings you strawberry lemonade when you asked for raspberry. Sure, it's perfectly fine to be internally a little irked by this, but it is not appropriate to cause a loud scene and yell about it. Even children would be scolded for such behavior. Instead, calmly talking to the server and explaining the mistake is a much more mature and civilized way of going about something like that.

However, let's change the scenario and say you're severely allergic to a particular ingredient—say, onions—and you explained that to a server. Well, when your dish arrives, it is covered with onions. Still, you should not raise your voice, but being a little sterner (yet still patient and kind), as your health or life may have been on the line, is more acceptable in such a situation.

In a nutshell, understanding and reading a room or situation before you react to something is a habit you should start getting into, if you haven't already. It's an integral part of being a young man because as you get older, you're going to be held more accountable for the way you act out in the world—and nobody (romantic partners, friends, coworkers, etc.) wants to be around someone who is impolite and rude to them and others.

1.2 THE ART OF SELF-CONTROL: KEEPING COOL UNDER PRESSURE

As I've already touched on in the previous section, being a competent and functioning young adult in society requires self-control in all aspects of your life—be it your reactions, the words you use, the way you treat other people, etc. In this section, I'll give you some coping mechanisms for controlling yourself in public and private.

Recognizing Pressure Points

Pressure points are specific parts of the body that are believed to be connected to other parts, such as regions and organs. By massaging them, a practice known as acupressure, you can sometimes relieve tension, pain, or stress in the corresponding sections. This goes for physical or emotional distress (but the emotional points are bolded).

Here are some commonly used pressure points for you to consider:

- SP-6 (Sanyinjiao): located four finger-widths above the ankle bone on the inside of the lower leg and engaged to relieve painful periods or menstrual cramps (sure, you may not directly benefit from this one, but you may have a girlfriend or platonic friend who might someday).

- P-6 (Neiguan): located on the inner forearm, three finger-widths away from your wrist, and activated to relieve nausea and prevent vomiting.

- ST-25 (Tianshu): located three finger-widths to the side of the belly button and stimulated to relieve constipation.

- ST-36 (Zusanli): located one hand-width under the knee on the outside of the lower leg and is thought to improve endurance and treat psychological conditions like stroke, pain, and hypertension.

- **LI-4 (Hegu):** located on the "meaty" part of your hand between the forefinger and thumb and often stimulated to relieve the pain of a migraine or tension headache and **to relieve stress.**

- **LV-3 (Taichong)**: located on the forefoot between the big toe and the next one and used to lower blood pressure, **reduce stress, and relieve anger and irritability.**

- Ren-6 (Qihai): located two inches below the belly button and activated to relieve constipation, gas, and bloating.

- **EX-HN3 (Yintang)**: also known as the "third eye," located between the eyebrows, and massaged to **help with symptoms of depression and anxiety**, as well as sinus headaches and pressure.

- LI-20 (Yingxiang): located in the folds on either side of your nose and may help relieve sinus pressure and nasal congestion.

- **(Circular motions on the top of your head and where the neck and shoulders meet can also reduce stress).**

But before you try to use pressure points, here are some things you need to consider:

- Please talk to your doctor about (and before starting) any new practices you're looking to incorporate into your daily wellness routine!

- Get in a comfortable position, take a few deep breaths, and relax your muscles.

- Use your thumb to push the pressure point for a few seconds at a time.

- Ongoing pressure or massage in small, circular strokes can also be effective.

- The pressure applied to each point should be firm but not too hard (stop the instant you feel pain).

- You should repeat consistent pressure until you find relief.

- If you find your fingers tire or hurt, you can always look for acupressure devices online.

Breathing and Counting Techniques

Breath work helps you release toxins as stress as you breathe out and nourish your mind and body when you breathe in. It has been found to help in the follow areas:

- Balancing blood pressure (whether too high or too low).

- Alkalizing your blood PH.

- Improving time spent in REM (deep) sleep.

- Reducing PTSD, anxiety, grief, and depression symptoms.

- Improving asthma symptoms.

- Promoting creativity.

- Increasing the function of your respiratory system.

- Improving immune systems.

- Releasing stress hormones.

- Elevating your mood.

- Decreasing addictive behaviors.

- Improving mental focus.

But there are many different kinds of breathwork techniques, including:

Deep Belly Breathing

This technique uses long, deep breath. As you inhale, you can picture your body filling up with air. Then, as you exhale, feel your chest relax and your belly button pull back. This exercise is a way for you to tell your body to relax. It can be used at any time—right before you give a big speech at school, get an injection at the doctor, are learning to drive, or anything else that makes you feel anxious.

Pursed Lip Breathing

This exercise reduces the number of breaths you take and keeps your airways open for a longer period of time. It's particularly helpful for athletes because they can be more physically active when more air is able to float in and out of their lungs. To practice, you just have to simply breathe in through your nose and breathe out twice as long through your mouth with pursed lips.

4-7-8 Breath

This one is similar to the deep belly breathing, but it adds the element of counting. So, you breathe in for four beats, hold for seven seconds, then breathe out for eight beats, and repeat. The longer exhale encourages you to completely empty your lungs and achieve a deeper sense of relaxation.

Alternate Nostril Breathing

Start with your right thumb applying pressure to your right nostril. Then, inhale with only your left nostril and hold in while you switch sides—placing your right pointer finger to apply pressure to the left nostril—and then only breathing through that side. This type of breathwork encourages the balance of your mind and body.

Lion's Breath.

This technique might feel kind of funny to do, but when done properly, it can relieve tension and stress in your face and chest. It involves breathing deeply through your nose, opening your eyes wide, opening your mouth and sticking your tongue out, to touch the tip down on your chin, and then letting the muscles in your throat contract as you exhale to make a "haaa" or roaring sound.

Holotropic Breathwork

It's best to work with an experienced instructor when first learning how to do this technique. However, the idea is to achieve a continuous inhale and exhale pattern with no pausing in between. This type of breathing floods your body with oxygen and renews your cells.

Sitali Breath

This is a breathing practice that helps lower your body temperature and relax your mind. To do it, you stick your tongue out and curl it, bringing the outer edges together (if your tongue doesn't do that, you can just purse your lips. Then, you inhale through your mouth and exhale through your nose.

Humming Bee Breath (Bhramari)

Similar to Lion's Breath, this technique involves exactly what it sounds like—you creating the sound of buzzing like a bee in your body. The unique sensation of which helps create a calmness throughout your body. In order to do it, you have to place your index fingers on the cartilage that partially covers your ear canal. Then, after inhaling, you press your fingers into the cartilage as you exhale while keeping your mouth closed and making a loud humming sound.

As with other practices I list in this book, please consult a doctor before you start any of them.

Long-Term Strategies

Like many lessons in life, learning self-control is Evergreen, meaning it is something you must continually practice and continue to get better at with time.

However, there are many things you can implement into your life that make self-control easier, including:

- Avoiding Temptation—We've already covered different triggers for emotions, but there are also events, desires, etc., that can set off our inability to control ourselves. For example, let's say you have an intense sweet tooth. Well, if you want to improve your diet, one of the best ways for you to eliminate sugary treats is by avoiding them in the store or going for a walk, calling a friend, or otherwise distracting yourself with a healthier activity can help. The goal is for you now to "use up" all of your self-control before you really need it.

- Planning Ahead—Similar to not buying sweets at the store, planning ahead to eliminate or minimize a negative behavior or habit can be very effective. Say you find that you suffer from intense afternoon hunger pangs. Well, a great way to reduce and avoid those, especially if you commonly reach for unhealthy snacks during those times, meal planning to have lunches filled with fiber, protein, and whole grains will assist you in staying fuller, from healthier food choices, longer.

- Focusing on One Goal—Setting several goals at once can cause overwhelm and lead you to ditch every single one. So, focusing on one at a time will help you reserve your resources once it becomes an effortless habit, and you can move onto working on the next. If you need help prioritizing your goals, try listing them all out and ranking them in a hierarchy. Whichever seems the most important (be it getting more sleep, making healthier diet choices, working out more, etc.) should be the first to work on. Or you can try to decide which ones will build on each other easily—like exercising every night, which will cause you to be tired and ready for bed earlier.

- Meditating—Being mindful and participating in meditation exercises, plenty of which you can find online, help you slow down your thoughts, which can aid in your ability to resist the gut impulses that can get in the way of your self-control.

- Remembering Consequences—As you learn that honing your self-control can help you achieve goals and improve your physical and mental health, you must also understand that a lack of self-control, on the other hand, can have adverse effects on your self-esteem and ability to succeed in school, have healthy relationships, and maintain well-being. Make sure to remind yourself of these consequences, especially when you feel like you're losing control, to help you stay motivated and on the path to success.

Learning from Experience

You'll likely find that time and experience will help your ability to control yourself easier, and that's because you'll learn from both your mistakes and your triumphs in doing so. For instance, try to think of a time when you truly and utterly lost control. Perhaps your team lost an important game or something else in your life didn't go the way you wanted it to. Say you had a complete temper tantrum in front of your family and friends. Even if that's never happened to you, try to at least imagine what that would feel like. Pretty terrible, right?

If that doesn't give you an accurate internal "ick," try thinking about how you've felt or would feel if you saw one of your teammates or classmates acting like that. Chances are you wouldn't have a lot of respect for that person.

Instead, people who handle upset with empathy (which we'll talk about shortly), grace, and poise, are much more respected in their communities.

So, the next time you're faced with a similar challenge, think to yourself, "Do I want to be *that* guy . . . the one who loses his cool? Or do I want to be the controlled and 'chill' guy who lets unimportant things roll off his shoulders?"

Of course, this is not to say that you can't express yourself. It's all about balancing scales. Some things, like the loss of a loved one or pet, are monumental and worth any means of grief you deem necessary—but be that at is may, you still have to be able to restrain yourself to societal standards. For example, it wouldn't be appropriate for you to throw chairs around or otherwise destroy your parents' house after hearing about such a loss. That's now how emotionally intelligent people act.

All of this may be hard to understand, and that's okay. If you feel like you could benefit from talking to a loved one* or a professional therapist to get a greater understanding, you should absolutely feel free from shame or guilt in doing so.

* If you're going to talk with a friend or family for advice, please make sure you're being careful in choosing who to confide in. You want to pick someone who has made choices in life and ended up in places that you want to emulate and occupy. For example, a brother or cousin who has gotten in trouble with the law for aggressive behavior might not be the best choice (unless they've made considerable measures to correct those impulses, of course). Just trust your gut. It'll tell you whether or not you've made a wise decision.

1.3 EMPATHY: WALKING IN SOMEONE ELSE'S SHOES

As you're getting closer and closer to becoming a young adult, you've likely already found that you need to empathize, meaning understanding and comparing the thoughts and feelings of others with your own. When you were a child, your often self-focused world didn't require such consideration. But adulthood is different. To function independently in the world, you must always consider others around you. This might sound exhausting, but it doesn't need to be.

The Basics of Empathy

As funny as it may seem, the foundation of empathy is thought to have both selfless *and* selfish intentions.

On the selfless side of things, empathy helps us cooperate with others, build friendships, make moral decisions (such as turning over cash you found on the floor of your local grocery store, returning someone's wallet, or shoveling your elderly neighbors' driveway, etc.), and intervene when we see another classmate being bullied.

However, on a selfish note, we instinctively learn to use others as "social antennas," meaning that we detect our own danger based on their behaviors and experiences. Think of our earliest ancestors. They had to rely heavily on their senses to create a mental model of intent when a new arrival showed up to their tribe. If the intent was malicious and deadly, for example, the sensitivity to pick up on that and warn others could be crucial and lifesaving.

Please also be aware that innately, many of us can be less willing or interested in empathizing with those who are of different religions, nationalities, races, genders, etc., than us. But these are the people who you will ultimately benefit from empathizing with the most because they raise your awareness and perspective (more on perspective shortly) on issues you may not have thoughtfully considered before.

Empathy vs. Sympathy vs. Compassion

While empathy, sympathy, and compassion are often used interchangeably, they actually aren't the same.

Sympathy is the feeling of concern for someone and the desire for them to become happier people. So, think of seeing someone clearly down on their luck holding up a sign indicating they are homeless and begging for money. The feelings you're probably experiencing in that instance is sympathy. Most people don't like to see others struggle, after all.

But empathy goes deeper than that and requires that we share another person's emotions. In order to be empathetic to the person experiencing homelessness, you must imagine what it would be like if *you* were going through that. How would you feel? Try to focus on the fear, the resentment, the anger, and the hopelessness you might experience.

Whereas compassion is defined as "the empathic understanding" of a person's feelings accompanied by a desire to act on one's behalf. So, giving the person we've been talking about here a few dollars would be a way of showing compassion. Or if you're a religious person, even muttering a quiet prayer could be your way of being compassionate. Whatever you believe you could do to help someone out is acting in compassion.

Listening Skills

Empathic listening is a process that requires more than just taking in someone's words. Instead, you must respond purposefully, indicating that you care about them, their thoughts, and their feelings.

Here are seven tips for empathic listening:

1. **Be nonjudgmental.** This isn't always the easiest practice, but when you learn to let go of your own opinions frees you up to focus on the other person's perspective. However, this does not mean that you have to agree with everything they say. It's just about letting them know you care about them, and that they matter to you.

2. **Give the person your undivided attention.** Especially in today's digital age, this can be tough, but giving your complete attention to someone involves removing all distractions, including screens or devices. This demonstrates a sense of respect.

3. **Listen carefully to feelings and facts.** In order to listen to someone empathically, you must do so with your ears, eyes, and heart. This means you have to not only observe and soak in the words being spoken, but also the person's tone of voice, body language, and other clues that go beyond words to gain insight on the other person's emotions.

4. **Show that you are listening carefully.** As you observe the other person's body language and nonverbal cues, you need to pay attention to your own as well. For instance, a good posture

is another way of showing your attention and respect to someone. Also, adding things in like making eye contact, nodding, and other signals can show your attentiveness without interrupting.

5. **Don't be afraid of silence.** In the same context of refraining from interruption, don't be afraid of silence, as it can indicate that the other person is either thinking about what they just said, deciding to say next, or just need a moment to rein in their emotions. So often, we get uncomfortable in the pauses between speaking, but often that quiet has context and quality.

6. **Restate and paraphrase.** If you do feel it's necessary or appropriate to respond with words, consider referring back to whatever they've said, asking questions, and/or clarifying comments. Remember to stay nonjudgmental and respectful. Of course, please also remember there's no "script" for this kind of listening, instead it's best to respond based on the person, situation, and the moment.

7. **Follow up.** The last step of empathic listening is following up with that person. See if they still feel the need to vent or ask questions. If so, set up another time to meet.

Empathic listening plays an important role in almost all of the relationships you'll have in life—be it with your roommates, your romantic partners, your close friends, your siblings, your parents, etc. It's how you show up and let people know you care about them.

Perspective-Taking

Exploring the perspectives of others will help you better understand experiences and viewpoints that differ from your own and build connections, empathize, and communicate with others.

It's also one of the best ways to learn about being the most effective advocate you can be for someone or a community of people.

If you feel you could use some guidance, here are a few strategies that can be helpful when perspective taking:

- Seek to understand—When engaging in conversations that are aimed at understanding different perspectives, try to set aside your personal goals and instead focus on the other person's experiences and their way of perceiving the world. (If this is difficult for you, try imagining how you'd want *them* to be open to your story.)

- Ask good questions—This again requires the removal of as much judgment as possible and asking questions that do not lead to particular responses and instead help you understand another person's viewpoint.

- Display empathy—As you're engaged in the conversation, strive to display welcoming body language, listen without verbal interruption, and validate their feelings when appropriate.

Further, there are several obstacles (think of them as "mind bugs" that can get in the way of you effectively listening) that you'll want to overcome while perspective taking, including:

- **Fundamental attribution error.** While we tend to blame others for the bad things that happen to them, we also tend to blame external situations when bad things happen to you. However, acknowledge and control over our own lives is one of the most powerful things we can do for ourselves and help others to do as well. (You know the saying that goes something like, "If you're always blaming others for being wrong, it's probably you that's wrong."?)

- **Naïve realism.** Often, we think that the world that we see objectively and "truly" is the same as other rational beings also see it. But that just simply isn't the case.

- **Intergroup bias.** We've already touched on this, but this refers to preferring members of your in-group and having prejudice against out-group members. Remember, this is natural but also incredibly dangerous way to think and live. You will remain forever pigeon-holed and unevolved if you do not seek the acquaintance and perspectives of people who are very different from you—and you might help them become more developed people as well!

- Confirmation bias. This is another natural yet hazardous way of thinking . . . we, as humans, often focus on the information that confirms our existing beliefs. This means we target that information while ignoring all of the rest. This will also almost assuredly limit your depth as a person.

Empathy in Action

Empathic action is the part of "doing" empathy. It goes beyond understanding others and listening to them sharing their thoughts, experiences, and feelings. It moves us to take action, and be compassionate, for others in any way we can.

As previously discussed, this can take many forms—be that directly helping, rallying for others to help, praying, or just sitting in silence with someone who you think could benefit from it.

But please be careful that empathic action does not always mean "fixing" the issue. Instead, you are simply standing in solidarity with someone or a group of people and acknowledging the change that needs to happen to benefit them. For example, volunteering at a local shelter isn't going to cure the issue of hunger and homelessness. But at least you're doing your part to help out around your community.

Another Warning

While empathy is incredibly important and beneficial, when it becomes your *default* mode, you can lose sight on your own needs. You know what they say on airplanes about putting your oxygen mask on before attempting to help others do the same? The same thing applies here. You cannot help others if you aren't first taking care of yourself.

Further, you also risk opening yourself up to being taken advantage of, which nobody likes experiencing, and to becoming "burnt out." So, make sure you're always taking little pauses to analyze the people you're surrounding yourself with. And if you need a little time of decompression, such as a night where you indulge in the finer things that you like in life (like a nice meal, a movie night, a day at the spa, etc., that's totally fine. But only you can know what limits and boundaries you need to put on yourself and others to stay mentally and physically healthy.

1.4 BUILDING RESILIENCE: BOUNCING BACK FROM SETBACKS

Yet another challenging aspect that comes with becoming a young man is dealing with resilience. Meaning, despite any setback you may experience, you can't crumble into the hysterics you may have resorted to as a child. Instead, in order to be a functioning member of society, you have to continue persevering, and hopefully learning, from anything—even the negative stuff—that may come your way.

It kind of seem unfair, right? Yeah. But such is life, unfortunately. But the sooner you realize that the better and easier your life will be. Remember, no matter how "perfect" someone's reality seems, it isn't. Everyone of is flawed and damages. However, it's what we do with that baggage that truly matters.

Understanding Resilience

Resilience is the process and outcome of successfully adapting to difficult or challenging life experiences, of which we all have at some point or another. The important thing is learning how, through our mental, emotional, and behavioral processes, to adjust to new external and internal demands that the world throws at us.

This adaptation is molded by several factors, such as the way in which you view and engage with the world, the availability and quality of your social resources (like therapists, guidance counselors, youth leaders at church, etc.), and your specific coping strategies.

In terms of coping strategies, psychologists have identified four ingredients that can help, including:

1. **Connection.** The connections you build and support between those in your community are extremely important as you navigate setbacks in life because they can remind you that you aren't alone in this world.

2. **Wellness.** Self-care is also important when dealing with stress because it isn't just emotional, it's also physical. So, prioritize your nutrition, sleep patterns, levels of hydration, and exercise routines. Moreover, you should also seek out hobbies—like mindfulness practices, journaling, drawing, yoga, or anything else that will help you express yourself.

3. **Healthy thinking.** We're going to touch on this below, but for now, just remember that your thoughts are like "spells," meaning that they shape your internal and external realities. So, you guessed it, they are very, very important and should be selected with care.

4. **Finding meaning and purpose.** Simply put, if you have a pulse, then you have a purpose. If it helps, seek out books, movies, etc., that focus on individuals who have struggled with similar (if not more significant) adversities than you. Then, sit down and try to map out small pieces of your problem that you can choose and focus on one at a time. This while hopefully show you that there's a light at the end of the tunnel—no matter what you're facing.

The Role of Optimism

As touched on above, positive thinking has a huge impact on our ability to be resilient and persevere in the face of adversity. Why? Well, because we wouldn't see any point in persistence if we didn't believe that there was something better waiting on the other side of it.

You see, without the optimism that our lives will only improve after we face a particular challenge, we'd just give up and never undertake anything difficult. Think about college, for instance. You're probably either just starting to think about it, or you're in the thick of deciding where you want to go (if at all) and what you want to do for a living. Sorry to say, but if you decide to go down that route, college isn't always easy.

But the reason why so many before you have endured the challenge is because there's a degree, and often a higher income potential and better quality of life waiting at the end of the journey.

Remembering the positives that come with hardships are a great way to put your head down, do the dirty work, and achieve your goals.

Learning from Failure

Given everything I've just said, it may seem counterproductive to think about, but it's true. Your failures can also teach you a great deal about resilience.

To get a better understanding of this, we're going to focus on an analogy posited by Martin E.P. Seligman in a podcast hosted and uploaded by *Harvard Business Review*. Seligman said that there were two men, one named Douglas and one named Walter, who were both University of Pennsylvania MBA graduates and both laid off their Wall Street jobs over a year ago.

At first, Douglas and Walter were both sad and scared about what their futures would hold.

But with time, Douglas decided to change his attitude. Instead of thinking, "Woe is me," he instead thought, "It's not me; it's the economy that's bad. I have plenty of skills, and there is a market for them."

This is all while Walter sunk deeper into his depression and thought things like, "I got laid off because I can't perform. I'm not cut out for the tough finance world."

I'm sure you've guessed it, but Douglas revamped his resume, took rejection after rejection from companies but never gave up hope until he found a position in his small Midwestern hometown. Walter, on the other hand, never looked for another job and moved back in with his parents.

So, Douglas and Walter stood at the two complete opposites of failure. Douglas sprung back into action after a period of feeling sorry for himself, and he only grew from the experiences, whereas Walter went from depression to a paralyzing fear of the future.

The important thing to remember here is that failure is inevitable in almost all areas of our lives—not just work, but also in romance, sports, anything. So, learning how to be a Douglas and thriving from it will ensure that you obtain the highest quality of life possible for you. Those who collapse from failure are the ones who truly fail.

1.5 SELF-REFLECTION: THE KEY TO PERSONAL GROWTH

Self-reflection requires you to sit, often in silence and while alone, and reflect on you are, how you feel or think about certain things, and what your behaviors are in accordance with those feelings or beliefs. An understanding of all the above can help you relate and communicate with others and find your place in the world.

The Importance of Self-Reflection

Logically, when we self-reflect, we also get a better understanding of our self-concept, which includes your thoughts about your natural or learned traits, abilities, beliefs, values, roles, and relationships.

Your self-concept also plays an influential role in your mood, judgment, and behavioral patterns.

And getting to know yourself is almost as important, if not more, than, say, getting a better understanding of your romantic partners, coworkers, friends, etc.

In addition, some of the benefits of self-reflection include:

- **Increased self-awareness.** Spending time in self-reflection increases your self-awareness, which is a key component of emotional intelligence because it helps you recognize and understand the impact of your emotions, thoughts, and behaviors.

- **Greater sense of control.** Self-reflection involves practicing mindfulness and being present with yourself at any given moment, which can help you feel more grounded and in control.

- **Improved communication skills.** Self-reflection also helps you improve your communication skills because the better you get at communicating with and understanding yourself, the easier it usually is for you to do so when it comes to others.

- **Deeper alignment with core values*.** As mentioned, self-reflection helps you understand what you believe and why, and that helps you ensure that your words and actions are aligned with each other (thus, avoiding cognitive dissonance, which occurs when your behavior doesn't line up with your values).

- **Better decision-making skills.** Understanding yourself better can help you evaluate all of your options in life and how they will impact you with more clarity.

- **Greater accountability.** Self-reflection can help you hold yourself accountable by evaluating your actions and recognizing your personal responsibility.

    * If you're unsure what your core values are, consider visiting websites like www.jamesclear.com/core-values, www.scottjeffrey.com/core-values-list, or any others that list values and decipher what your top ten are. Then, play a game that involves reducing one by one until you get down to three. Then, those three values are your most important (although they can change as you deem fit) and should be the basis you work off of.

Journaling Techniques

Quite simply, a reflective journal is a place to write down your daily, weekly, etc., reflection entries. It can be a notebook, notepad, Word document, or anywhere else you feel comfortable writing down the positive and negative things that happened to you, what you learned about yourself through them, and anything else you feel like memorializing.

In general, there are three effective steps to write reflectively:

1. **What?** (Description.) Recall an event and write it down descriptively.

   What happened? Who was involved?

2. **So what?** (Interpretation.) Take a few minutes and interpret the event.

   What is the most important/interesting/useful aspect of the event, idea or situation? How can it be explained? How is it similar or different from others that you've experienced?

3. **What's next?** (Outcome.) Conclude what you could learn from the event and how you can apply it next time.

   What have I learned? How can it be applied in the future?

In addition, here are ten writing prompts that you can use to get you started in a reflective journal:

1. What makes you unique?
2. Name someone that means a lot to you and why.
3. Write a letter to your younger self.
4. What is something you can do to focus more on your health and overall well-being?
5. What makes you feel at peace?
6. List ten things that make you smile.
7. What does it mean to you to live authentically?
8. What is your favorite animal, and why?
9. How do you maintain your physical and mental health?
10. List the things you want to achieve this week. This month? This year?

And you can use these prompts over and over again because the answers may change depending on where you're at or facing in life.

Feedback from Others

Whether we like it or not, we also have to take into consideration feedback from those around us when engaging in self-reflection. For instance, in school, we rely on teachers to teach us, grade us, and provide us with guidance and support in ways for us to succeed.

However, it's important to note that feedback is actually a two-way street. It's not only how someone else provides guidance to us, but it's also about how we *receive* it. As long as it's helpful, strong, and constructive, feedback is a great way for us to understand ourselves and grow as people. Moreover, good feedback should also be timely, specific, and focused on results or a particular behavior.

In particular, feedback is important in terms of self-reflection because there are often gaps in the way we see ourselves and how others do. So, feedback can help fill those gaps in understanding our reputations, where we excel, and where we could work to improve ourselves. All of that helps us to discover the best versions of ourselves that we can be.

If it'll help, consider going back to your

When Self-Reflection Harms

We've discussed all of the benefits of self-reflection, but just with almost anything in life, there are also downsides.

Please consider changing your tune or speaking with a trusted family member, friend, or therapist if you experience the following when reflecting on yourself:

- **Rumination.** This occurs when you have excessive or repetitive stressful or negative thoughts that interferes with other parts of your life and mental activity.

- **Self-judgment.** This is a little tricky because it is healthy to judge yourself, in terms of your treatment of others, work toward your goals, etc. But when it becomes a constant thing—especially if you're always focusing on what others have that you lack—it can be very harmful to your mental well-being.

- **Negative self-talk.** This occurs when you allow the little voice inside your head to negatively impact your life. Typically, it tells you that you aren't good enough or capable of accomplishing the things you want to do. Remember that your thoughts are just that . . . thoughts. And they are only given meaning and power when you allow them to. Instead, it's much more effective to switch your frame of thought to something more positive.

- **Comparison.** You've probably already heard this before, but it's true: comparison is the thief of all joy. So, when you notice your mind starting to compare yourself to others, in terms of looks, grades, romantic options, etc., try your best to recenter and focus on all of the amazing things you have going for you.

1.6 SUMMARY

An important part of becoming a young adult is gaining emotional intelligence, which means learning to navigate and control your emotions, thoughts, and behaviors, be empathetic towards others, be resilient in times of strife and hardship, and be able to self-reflect and get a deeper understanding of who you are and what your goals are.

It may seem daunting, and that's because, at times, it is. And it's an ongoing process that requires time, dedication, and tenacity.

But keep at it! Hopefully this book has provided you with a good foundation and curiosity to go out there and continue learning how to better yourself. Your older self will only thank you for the work you put into it now as a teenager.

CHAPTER TWO:
SELF-IDENTITY AND CONFIDENCE

2.1 DISCOVERING WHO YOU ARE: BEYOND LABELS AND STEREOTYPES

I've already covered self-reflection, but this chapter will go even further into self-discovery and provide you with tools to build your confidence, mental fortitude, boundaries, and overall image of the unique and awesome person you are.

Peeling Back the Layers

As we've said, one of the best ways to discover who you are is by determine *what* you want out of life. This is especially important for someone your age because you really need to hone and consider the goals you want to accomplish in life.

For example, you may be fine acting like the high school student you've come to know and be comfortable with, but depending on where you're going in the future, you may need to morph and transform accordingly. Perhaps you are the captain of your high school's football team, and that's been your primary identity. Well, that's all fine as well as long as you're still in high school and playing that sport.

However, as you enter college, trade school, or go right into the work force, you can't be that person anymore. Sure, you're still Brad, John, or Eric, but you are no longer the captain of your football team. Instead, you're the science major, the aspiring mechanic, the salesman, etc. All of those personas and goals are going to come with different ways of "being" in order to be successful.

Values and Beliefs

It bears repeating that one of the first places you should work from when discerning the person you are and want to be is by deciding what values and beliefs are most important and crucial in accomplishing your goals.

Here are a few examples:

Goal #1: To be a doctor.

>Necessary values and beliefs: education, knowledge, professionalism, responsibility, wealth, authority, and accountability.

Goal #2: To sell cars.

> Necessary values and beliefs: Friendliness, charisma, knowledge, authority, relatability, and positivity.

Goal #3: To be a reporter.

> Necessary values and beliefs: Punctuality, professionalism, sociability, trustworthiness, and reliability.

Goal #4: To be an entrepreneur.

> Necessary values and beliefs: Hard work, creativity, abundance, ambition, charisma, knowledge, independence, and power.

These are just examples, and even if you share any of the goals above, the values and beliefs you believe that you'll need to accomplish them will probably look different. But hopefully these got you to understand where I'm coming from.

Above all else, please just remember that in order to "do" someone who achieves the goals that you want to, you must first decipher your ability *and* desire to "be" that kind of person.

If it will help, go back and decipher your goals through the exercise listed under 1.5. That may help you narrow down the direction/career you want (and also don't want) to pursue in the future.

Interests and Passions

Of course, one of the more obvious places to look at when trying to find who you are or want to be in the future (and, in general, there shouldn't be a huge discrepancy between the two because you want to work from your natural talents and gifts), it's important to look at your interests and passions.

This doesn't only go for your future schooling and career. It's also about your personal goals in terms of health and exercise, your goals for a romantic partner and a family, etc.

In terms of the latter, it might seem like you're too young to even be considering that kind of thing, but it actually isn't. The choices you make today can have a huge impact on all aspects of your future.

For example, let's say you see yourself as a successful police officer with a partner/spouse and several kids by the time you're twenty-five. Now, of course, those goals can change. But if that's where you see yourself going now, it is not in your best interest to get bogged down by illegal things like drugs, alcohol, or truancy issues, right now. Again, I know your future seems lightyears away, but trust me, your past will follow you anywhere you go.

Another example would be if you want to become a fashion designer but feel like a few years interning in Italy or Paris, for instance, will help you develop your artistic vision . . . well, in that case, starting a traditional four-year program right out of school at a typical college might not be aligned with your dreams.

What I'm trying to say, and I hope you're getting, is that it's never too early to consider and start planning for your future based on who you are and who you want to be and the goals you hope to achieve (professionally and personally).

Overcoming Societal Expectations

Unfortunately, and this can be really tough, deciding to go down a different path than what your parents, grandparents, siblings, or society as a whole seemed to expect from you can be hard—especially when you feel like you're disappointing your loved ones.

But as long as your goals are positive and add to society for the good, fill you with joy, and make you feel like you're living out your unique life's purpose, please hold fast and true to them. This is not to say that you can't change them, but the changes, if any, should come from inside of you—not from external sources.

If you need inspiration, think of all the people who have seemed to accomplish the impossible—like those who have won Nobel Peace prizes, Olympic medals, Grammy awards, you name it. Guaranteed almost all of them had people in their lives who doubted them and said they couldn't do it.

2.2 CONFIDENCE BUILDING 101: OVERCOMING SELF-DOUBT

We've just mentioned people throughout history who have gone on to accomplish incredible accolades, but I'm sure even they have struggled with feelings of self-doubt. Unfortunately, that's also one of those annoying yet normal parts of human nature. From time to time, we all experience doubt in ourselves. But the real challenge is not giving into it and persevering through it (another part way of being resilient!).

Identifying Sources of Self-Doubt

First of all, lets dig into what it means to have self-doubt. As you'd expect, it refers to thoughts and feelings someone has about their abilities to achieve of concur something. However, it can also refer to unrealistic thoughts people have about their abilities to achieve something.

Basically, self-doubt involves varying thoughts and judgments about one's own abilities.

So, what is the opposite of self-doubt? It's a person's ability to know what to expect from their performance—be that good, bad, or somewhere in the middle. Of course, it's never definite, as, for example, people competing in the Olympics can benefit from adrenaline rushes and other advantages to peek their performances, but likely, at the end of race or event, that athlete at least knew the likely confines of where they'd land on the scoreboard.

In attempting to identify your self-doubts, you can consider the following questions and scales:

"More often than not, I feel unsure of my abilities to _____." Fill in the gap based on your passions, interests, and goals. So, you could put draw, sew, play football, cook, study, perform advanced science experiments, etc.

Strongly disagree   Strongly agree

1 2 3 4 5 6 7 8 9 10

"As I begin an important activity, I usually feel confident in the likely outcome."

Strongly disagree   Strongly agree

1 2 3 4 5 6 7 8 9 10

The higher your scores are, the less self-doubt you have, and vice versa for lower scores.

Positive Affirmations

A great and powerful tool for breaking out of self-doubt is the adoption and repetition of positive affirmations, which are words or sentences that you can say in order to manifest and change the way you subconsciously think about something.

In terms of self-doubt, you can try some* of the following (or make up your own!):

- I know what I'm capable of.

- I deserve good things.

- I learn from my past and shape my future accordingly.

- Great success is waiting for me.

- I deserve joy, success, and abundance.

- Fear doesn't hold me back from anything.

- I can achieve all of my goals and reach all of my dreams.

- I always fall on my feet.

- I don't settle for more than I deserve.

By repeating these positive mantras, you are actually training your brain to believe them and turn them into reality! It's honestly like magic (remember what I said earlier about words being like spells.).

* Try not to overwhelm yourself with too many mantras or affirmations, however. Limit them to the ones that are especially important to you at a specific point in your life.

Surrounding Yourself with Positivity

Other than thinking positively, it's also essential as you grow into young adulthood that you surround yourself with positive human beings who support you, raise you up, and have similar morals, beliefs, and values as you.

These are the kind of people you want to always surround yourself with while also supporting their dreams and goals.

Together, you'll hold each other accountable and see each other's lives develop into whatever you dreamed they'd be. Again, this is not to say that anyone's life turns out perfect, that couldn't be further from the truth. But in general, as long as you hold true and loyal to your goals, they'll find a way of coming true.

2.3 THE POWER OF POSITIVE SELF-TALK

I hope you're really understanding how important the way you talk to yourself, either out loud or just in your head, is to your development, or lack thereof, in life.

So, just as essential the process of positive self-talk is to recognize and practice, it's also key to understand and realize when you're engaging in negative self-talk.

Recognizing Negative Self-Talk

It may be easier said than done but, in general, you should know you're engaging in negative self-talk when you *feel* discomfort.

When you're feeling anger, anxiety, stress, frustration, hopelessness, sorrow, etc., you're more than likely telling yourself a "sad" story you're sick, you're going to get a bad grade in whatever class, the person you've had a crush on will never like you back, you're never going to get into the school you want to get into, etc., are all examples of thoughts and feelings you can have that stunt your growth and potential.

Changing the Narrative

Also, easier said than done, and something that requires constant attention and practice is changing your negative thought and recognizing four things:

1. Your thought is simply something that's rattling around in your brain.

2. You are actually in control of your thoughts and what goes on in your mind.

3. So, instead of thinking _____, I want to think _____ (the exact opposite).

4. Then, repeat that new, positive mantra over and over again.

Once this process becomes a habit, you'll find things changing for the better all around you. However, don't feel bad if you slip up from time to time. That's perfectly normal. Just start from step one and repeat them over and over again.

The Role of Self-Compassion

We've already gone over the compassion you need to have for others, but did you know that it's also important for you to have for yourself? Oh, yes. At the end of the day, we're all flawed humans who are learning our lessons.

No matter how hard we try, we'll never be perfect. That isn't attainable or even possible. Instead, as long as we can rest our heads on our pillows at the end of the day knowing we did the best we could, were the kindest people we could be, and lived as much in alignment with our goals and beliefs as we could that day, then we've done a pretty good job!

Also, please do your best to remember that everyone—and I mean everyone—slips up, loses their cool, acts impatient, and says or does something they regret. What's important is that you learn from your mistakes going forward and act differently the next time a similar situation arises.

Practicing Gratitude

I've gone over manifestation already, but did you know that you cannot manifest or attract more of whatever it is that you already have, take advantage of, or do not appreciate? It's true. Whether you believe in a higher power such as God, the universe, or anything else, it is that source that provides for you.

So, when you live your day thinking in lack . . . that's what you're telling the world you want more of.

Consider this the next time you're roaming the halls and observing the coolest shoes another guy has on that you wish you had. Is that thinking in gratitude? No! If you were being grateful, you'd be thanking God, the universe, whatever, that you have shoes on your feet when you know that so many other people have to suffer from walking barefoot on hot sand and cement. Do you see the difference there?

Another great, and easily missed, example of how blessed you are is whether or not you have clean, drinkable water running from your faucet or easily accessible in your home or school. Do you know how many people around the world do not have that luxury? Please, the next time you take a drink from a water fountain or fill up your water bottle, thank your lucky stars that you're so fortunate to be able to do so with such ease.

If you find it helpful, you can also purchase or start a gratitude journal. This will give you a place to reflect on the similar things in life that so many of us take for granted.

2.4 SETTING PERSONAL BOUNDARIES: LEARNING TO SAY NO

In developing autonomy and independence as a young adult, you should also start thinking about and establishing boundaries between others around you. These may seem selfish at times, but if they are important to you and your goals, you should try your best to hold firm with them.

The Importance of Boundaries

Establishing boundaries is how we communicate to others about what is or isn't okay behavior and conduct from our friends, coworkers, romantic interests, and family members*.

It might be hard for you to comprehend your ability to have these at your age, but please know that you have every right as anyone else older than you to demand respect for your mental, physical, sexual, intellectual, emotional, and financial well-being.

* With family members, especially our parents or guardians, siblings, aunts and uncles, etc., it's often seen as disrespectful to go against their demands and wishes—but if you feel like anything they're asking of you invades a boundary, try talking to them calmly about it, if you think you're safe to do that. Otherwise, consider approaching a guidance counselor or other trusted adult. It might be hard to talk about, but that's okay. At any age, you should not feel exploited or taken advantage of.

Identifying Your Boundaries

Before establishing a boundary, please take the time to reflect on your needs, struggles, and how it's impacting your relationship.

Let's say your volleyball coach is insisting on additional practices that are making you, and likely others, fall back on coursework and sleep. In that case, your first step, depending on the kind of person your coach is, would be to sit them down and calmly assert that the extra practices are detrimental to your grades, which is unacceptable to you. Well, hopefully, they will be amenable to that and change the schedule accordingly. However, if the coach is not as reasonable as that, you, and potentially other teammates, may have to go into the principal's office and explain the situation.

Whatever your necessary boundary, please know that there's always someone you can go to for help—and starting with a guidance counselor or other trusted adult is a great place to start for guidance and advice about how to navigate that situation.

However, it's also important for you to be aware that sometimes commitments you make, like being on the volleyball team, that may come with extra practice time when state competitions come around, are sometimes non-negotiable, and the result may need to be for you not to participate anymore.

Unfortunately, with a lot of things we cover in this book, there are gives and pulls to most situations. But as I said, there are some aspects in your life, and if you don't know what they are, please talk with a counselor or therapist for clarity, that should never, ever be violated.

Communicating Boundaries

Regardless of your gender, a boundary can be established by the complete sentence of, "N-o." However, if you can, expressing them in a way that makes the person you're communicating with feel respected and treated with kindness is best, when applicable.

If you struggle when communicating your boundaries, please try to remind yourself that you're establishing them in an effort to support, build, and maintain relationships with people.

As alluded to before, if the relationship between you and someone you need to communicate a boundary to involves a power dynamic, you may especially consider reaching out for additional support.

2.5 EMBRACING YOUR UNIQUENESS: CELEBRATING INDIVIDUALITY

One of the coolest things about being a human on this earth is that we're all different in our own respects. But what does that mean? We'll discover that further in this section.

What Makes You Unique

Again, it depends on what higher presence you believe in, if any, but many believe that you were put on this planet to occupy a very specific purpose that is completely unique to you.

You may have heard from others that your looks or mannerisms remind them of a friend or family member that they have, but what you likely haven't heard is that you're *exactly* like another person. And that's because it probably isn't true!

Think about it, even you and your best friend, no matter how compatible or similar you may be, there are probably even more wonderful things that make you different—some of the music you like, your favorite subjects in school, your all-time favorite movie, your taste in a significant other, your love language, etc.

The Strength in Diversity

A huge benefit of everyone coming into industries, projects, and cases having different perspectives, personalities, and natural talents, is that such diversity leads to change and innovation. If we all felt, thought, and cared about the same things, we'd never bring new ideas or ways of doing things to the table.

Furthermore, diversity aids in problem solving, creating equity, which is the quality of being fair and impartial, and maintaining democracy, due to the fact that members of diverse groups feel they have a voice, vote, and a choice.

Overcoming the Fear of Judgment

Something that can tempt us to conform and hold back our true selves is the fear of judgment from others who are not like us.

Unfortunately, there isn't necessarily a "quick fix" to getting over this. However, there are certain things you can do in order to move toward overcoming the fear of judgment, including:

- **Joining a support group.** Although this may seem intimidating at first, group therapy is an effective way for some to feel safe in a supportive environment to practice social interactions, cope with anxiety, and build confidence. Moreover, it can be beneficial to hear from others who struggle with similar problems as you do.

- **Challenging your thoughts.** It's often helpful for people to remember that others are like them and more preoccupied in their own lives to give a whole lot of thought to your behavior, fashion sense, vocal tones, hairstyle, or anything else you might be concerned about being judged over. Think about it—how much time to devote to thinking about or even noticing those around you?

- **Meditate or practice mindfulness.** As you understand and come to terms with who you are as a person, the more likely it will be that you're comfortable with that. Furthermore, such practices may also help calm you down before social interactions that would otherwise cause you anxiety and/or stress.

- **Celebrate the difference in others.** This might seem contrary to the second bullet point, but it really isn't. At the same time as you may be more preoccupied with your own comings and goings, as is human nature, you can also take the conscientious time to take a break, observe someone with a different race, religion, cultural influence, fashion sense, etc., and trying your best to respectfully celebrate them is a way of putting good vibes into the karmic universe. By celebrating others, you are promoting the celebration of your own unique background and sensibilities.

2.6 SUMMARY

As a whole, our world will only become a better place when we all embrace our own unique takes, personalities, and interests while also celebrating the differences of other people. But in order to do that, we much first decipher who we are, overcome self-doubt, learn to say no when appropriate, establish boundaries, and accept ourselves and others.

Like many aspects in this book, self-acceptance and exploration is often a life-long journey. But when done right, it can be exciting, enticing, and riveting.

CHAPTER THREE:
MAKING AND MAINTAINING FRIENDSHIPS

Right now, your friends might be people you've known your entire life and were brought into your life based on circumstance—such as living near you, having the same classes, being on your football team, etc.

But as your social world expands and you get your first job or do whatever else you want or need to do outside of school, you're going to need to know how to make new friends.

This chapter will help you navigate ways to do that while also giving you tips and tricks for maintaining your old friendships.

3.1 FINDING YOUR TRIBE: MAKING NEW FRIENDS

For those who haven't had to bond with people outside of their main circle of friends, this can be really daunting. You may not know what to say, who to trust, or how to maintain professional boundaries, when necessary. But don't worry. We've got you covered.

And even if you've moved around a lot, for example, you will still benefit from considering the following information.

Opening Up to New Experiences

I was a little older than you, but when I was in college, I had a month-long internship in India. It was the first time I ever traveled abroad, and I did it all by myself. It was terrifying, but one thing I decided even before stepping on the plane was that I would say "yes" to anything, as long as it was safe and affordable, someone staying at the same hostel asked if I wanted to do.

Travel to the Taj Mahal? Yes. Visit an elephant village and teach a lesson to the children who live there? You betcha! Attend a fashion and dance show? Yep. Go into the local market? Uh-huh. I'm sure you're getting it by now.

By being open to these experiences, I made bonds and made memories I never would have if I just stayed in the comfortable confines of my room (or wasn't brave enough to make the trip at all).

Now, you may not be tackling something as major as traveling across the world, but even when starting a new job or sport, it's important that you're open and willing to make friends, and that often requires you to stick your neck out, share tidbits about yourself, and participate in activities with or teammates and colleagues outside of practice or work.

But remember, only participate in things that align with your morals, beliefs, and goals. Being open does not mean changing who you are.

The Role of Extracurricular Activities

As touched upon above, finding people who share in your interests is a great way to make new friends. If you're into sports, for example, joining your high school's team or trying to find intermural or rec team might be in your best interest.

Plus, aside from making new friends, such activity will also look good on a college or job application in the future!

Online Communities

Similar to extracurricular activities, you can also reach out to online communities who share interests with you.

However, please be incredibly careful here. Don't overshare about details of your life, and you should never, ever meet up with someone you've never spoken to over the phone or seen during videocalls. Further, absolutely and under no circumstances, should you go out to meet anyone you've never met before alone and/or in a private location.

When being a part of an online forum or chat room, please always keep it in the back of your mind there are bad people in the world who would jump at the chance to take advantage of you—regardless of your age or gender. We tend to think of girls and women being susceptible, and while that's true, you are too. Protect yourself.

Moreover, it's probably a good idea if you let your parent or another trusted adult review the people you're interacting with online and their comments to you. It's not that you're naïve, but you are still a kid, and something might be said that you don't recognize as being problematic.

3.2 THE ART OF CONVERSATION: BEYOND SMALL TALK

Once you've established a sense of trust with someone, you should probably start divulging more information about yourself to them—as they'll likely start doing to you. For some, especially those of us who are more introverted, this can seem scary. But it doesn't have to be. Promise!

Mastering Small Talk

Small talk, i.e., light, informal conversation between people who don't know each other that well, is something that many would rather not engage in, but it's actually really important—especially as new relationships and friendships are forming.

Here are a few tricks to consider if you find yourself struggling with small talk:

- **Practice it everywhere.** Like with anything else in life, you can't get better at small talk unless you practice. So, taking every opportunity to small talk with people—be it at church, your job, school, wherever—will help you improve and become more comfortable speaking like this.

- **Stop trying to be interesting and start being interested.** It can take the pressure off of small talk when you truly focus on learning about the other person instead of worrying about "selling yourself." Asking them meaningful and appropriate questions about their interests and actually listening to the answers, instead of focusing on what you're going to say about yourself, is a great way to get to know people.

- **Ask the right questions.** It can be off-putting to someone if you come out of left field and ask them something that's unrelated to your current situation. So, asking questions about how they know the host of the party you're at, for example, would be a great way to start a conversation with a stranger.

- **Build on or branch out of the small talk.** Once you've established a conversation, through the question about the host of the party, from the last bullet point, for instance, you must also consider how to branch off into other relevant topics. If they say work is what brought them and the host together, additional lines of questioning could be: what they do for work, how long they've been friends, etc.

- **Avoid controversial topics.** Things like politics, death, conspiracy theories, and religion, are often off-limits for your first few interactions with people. Of course, there are exceptions, especially given the situation you're in—for instance, if you meet at church, perhaps religion would be an acceptable topic of conversation. But this is just generally speaking and envisioning you meeting someone out in the wild (like at a dinner party, grocery store, etc.).

- **Don't be afraid to leave if the small talk is uncomfortable.** Unfortunately, sometimes you just don't jive with people. It happens to every single one of us. So, if you ever find yourself trying to engage with someone who is anti-social or just uninterested, excusing yourself politely is perfectly fine. Saying something like, "Nice chatting with you. But I'm going to get back to my friends. See you around." should do the trick without offending anyone.

Active Listening

You'll learn more about this in the following chapter, but for now, all you need to know about active listening is that it requires you to do exactly what it sounds like . . . listen. That means you aren't fiddling with your phone or another distraction. Instead, you're giving your undivided attention to someone and what they're saying.

Further, you also want to avoid too many interruptions but still communicate your involvement in the conversation by nodding or saying things like, "Right," "I understand," etc., at the appropriate times.

Asking Open-Ended Questions

You've probably heard someone in your life talk about how important the who, what, how, why, and when are. And that's because they're the starting points for collecting important information about a situation or person.

When it comes to a person, asking such open-ended questions gives them encouragement to continue speaking with you because you're giving them a "board" to dive off of, so to speak. This makes the conversation easier for both of you.

Conversational Etiquette

Other than the things like avoiding controversial topics and actively listening to others, that we've already covered, you should also be careful to address those older than you with respectful titles, such as Mr. or Mrs. ____, sir and ma'am, etc., always say "please" and "thank you", observe your non-verbal cues, and just be respectful of others whenever you can.

3.3 DEALING WITH CONFLICT: HEALTHY RESOLUTIONS

If you spend enough time with anyone, you're likely going to have a conflict with them. That's because we're all different people with varying opinions, ideas, perspectives, beliefs, and desires.

But as long as you take the time and care to learn from each disagreement you have with someone, you will likely only be better for it. Not only will you have a better understanding of your particular view on something, but you'll also have the added knowledge of theirs as well, which may alter your perspective or double-down on your own even more.

It's also through arguments that you truly learn who people are on the inside. Have you ever heard of the saying, "When someone tells them who you are, you should believe them?" It's so incredibly true and important.

Identifying the Source of Conflict

More often than not, sometimes our friends, classmates, teammates, and coworkers just get on our nerves, and that can lead us to say or do things that incite an argument or tension. However, you should be careful to assess what the actual source of that annoyance was to move on and grow.

For example, was it a non-verbal, like chewing gum loudly, or a physical action, like shoving someone in the hallway, that made you irritable in the first place? For something as non-offensive as smacking gum, you can just chalk that up to bad manners. But for inappropriate and rude behavior like shoving someone, you may want to consider whether or not that's someone you want to be friends with in the first place.

Let's consider a workplace environment. Say you have heated words with a fellow McDonald's employee. Take a step back and see what caused them. Was it that you think they're lazy and require you to do more work in order to make up for that? Or, again, were you simply having an off day? Your follow-up moves will vary wildly given your conclusion.

Effective Communication Skills

You'll also learn more about this in the next chapter but in terms of effective communication with your family. However, the concepts are the same for your friends and include:

- **Speaking clearly and concisely.** Using "um", "uh", or other "filler words" often take away from your message and your sense of authority.

- **Preparing ahead of time.** This is similar to the first point, but it also requires you to think through a conversation from start to finish. Of course, the real talk with your friend will never go exactly as you planned, but thinking about the possible ways in which it might go will help you anticipate the otherwise unexpected.

- **Being mindful of non-verbal communication**. Doing things like rolling your eyes, or crossing your arms have a significantly bigger impact on the person you're talking to than your actual words, and, therefore, they communicate much more too.

- **Watching your tone.** Like non-verbal communication, the way in which you say something (including your volume, projection, and intonation*) can also have a huge impact on the way your words are interpreted and received. In general, your tone when speaking should match the goal of your conversation.

* The rise and fall of your voice.

Forgiveness and Moving Forward

In general, forgiveness is hard and complicated. One reason for that is because it comes with a level of vulnerability. If you forgive someone, are you opening yourself up to being hurt all over again by them? It's hard to say.

But one benefit of forgiveness is that you don't actually have to voice it to the person who upset or hurt you—regardless of whether or not you ever speak to them again. Instead, if you choose to keep it for yourself, which absolutely is the right decision in some cases, then you're forgiving based on your own mental and emotional well-being.

Here are six steps to consider when going through the process of forgiveness:

1. Acknowledge your feelings and allow you to feel them (for as long as you deem necessary and appropriate).

2. Try to understand the other person's perspective and communicate that with them (if possible).

3. Set boundaries going forward (again whether or not you continue the friendship or not—and with only yourself or the other person as well).

4. Focus on yourself and your own well-being.

5. When you're ready, consciously let go of the negative feelings and emotions tied to the situation.

3.4 BEING A GOOD FRIEND: SUPPORT AND TRUST

A good friendship is all about equal give and take. As much love, support, and trust you have for and in someone else, you should feel that they have just as much for you. That's what true friendship is.

The Pillars of Friendship

In general, there are seven pillars of friendship. And they include:

1. **Encouragement and celebration.** A friend is someone who celebrates our triumphs and has encouraged us all along to achieve them.

2. **Forgiveness and comprehension.** Friends are people who forgive us (to a point) and help and stick with us during times of turmoil in life.

3. **Trust and truth.** Just as you want a friend who will be brutally honest with you, you should expect to be the same way for your friend. Someone who goes along with everything you say or do

is not a true friend because they likely aren't looking out for your best interest.

4. **Assertiveness and maintenance.** Typically, friends are people who you have selected carefully and worked hard to maintain a close relationship with.

5. **Responsibility and morality.** If you find it hard to keep your word with someone, or you believe they're struggling with keeping theirs with you, you may want to reevaluate the situation. You should want to spend time with your friends (and vice versa).

6. **Gratitude and Appreciation.** You should never take advantage of a good friend, and you similarly should never feel taken advantage of in a friendship.

7. **Solace and tomfoolery.** You know you have a good friend when you are comfortable being completely silent and also engaging in fun, silly behavior. Life is about a balance of both, and so should your friendships.

Showing Empathy and Support

This section may be able to go without saying, but in order to show support and empathy for your friends, you just have to simply be there for them—physically, when possible, but also emotionally.

As mentioned, you should take the time to check in with your friends, and they should do the same for you, both in happy and in sad, stressful times. Also, you should mutually and genuinely care for each other. That means it isn't often seen as a drag or an inconvenience to set a few moments aside to call, text, or chat in person.

However, in order to be a good friend, you must also respect boundaries in contact that your friend might establish (full time or temporarily). Remember what I said about my buddy when he was a new father? It wasn't necessarily a verbal boundary he put on me, but we also had a mutual understanding that I'd back away from contact, and he'd hit me if he needed me. I knew he needed that time to focus on his family. Acknowledging boundaries and limitations is also a way of showing respect and support.

3.5 NAVIGATING PEER PRESSURE: STAYING TRUE TO YOURSELF

When evaluating your friendships, you should also consider whether or not someone helps or hinders you in being the best version of yourself possible. That means not enticing or bullying you into things (like drugs, shoplifting, drinking, etc.) that will only distract you from your goals.

Understanding Peer Pressure

Simply put, peer pressure is an action or behavior taken upon by someone your age with the desired outcome of making you do something* you don't want to do or otherwise wouldn't do.

It can come in the form of teasing you for not doing something, trying to encourage you to do it, or trying to shove you out of friend groups (like ignoring you or treating you like an outcast).

* Please also know that peer pressure isn't *always* a bad thing. When done to positively affect your life (such as encouraging you to try out for a sports team or getting stricter with your studies, for example), it can change your life for the better. But we're focusing more on negative outcomes for the purposes of this book.

Confidence in Decision-Making

This is especially true as you get older because you're going to be held more and more to your decisions (both personally and by others). So, please do not make them lightly. Meaning, you should sit down and really think what you want in your life and then make big and small decisions accordingly.

However, if you're encountered with a decision you didn't anticipate or previously consider, one of the best ways for you to know which one to make is to sit with the feelings of each option.

The ones that make you feel bad are probably not for you, while those that make you happy and even proud of yourself, are the ones you should lean into making.

For instance, you're at a friend's house when his older brother's friends come into the basement or room with weed, and you're offered a joint. You never thought you'd have to make that decision that night—it just *happened.* Well, is taking a hit of it something that you feel good about? Hopefully not. Instead, politely declining before either asking your friends to leave or just leaving by yourself, is the better option.

The Power of "No"

When coming from you or offered to you, "No" is a full sentence. You don't need to say more, and you shouldn't expect anything else from another person after that's uttered.

So, if you're feeling pressured into an activity that doesn't align with your beliefs and morals, this two-lettered word is all you need to say. It's powerful and communicates a lot more than some may think.

If someone offers you drugs, and you say no, you don't need to elaborate on why you don't want to do them.

Similarly, if someone invites you to a party where you know drinking is going to be taking place, you can say no without any further explanation. Even if they ask things like, "Why?" or "Are you scared?" you don't have to say anything if you don't want to.

3.6 SUMMARY

Friendship is a wonderful thing, but it doesn't come without hard work, maintenance, and mutual respect.

Further, if you feel like you're in a friendship at any time that is one-sided or with someone whose morals, values, and beliefs do not align with yours, you should always feel the freedom to move on from it. I promise there are people around you who will be willing and able to fill the gap.

CHAPTER FOUR:
UNDERSTANDING FAMILY DYNAMICS

Family is defined by *Oxford Languages* as "a group of one or more parents and their children living together as a unit" and "all the descendants of a common ancestor." But a family is so much more than that. For instance, your family can include those that you share blood with, who you have intense and trusting emotional bonds with, or anyone else you feel positively impacts your life. We'll dive into almost every kind of family in this next chapter.

4.1 FAMILY ROLES: UNDERSTANDING EACH OTHER

Family roles dictate how we interact with others and function to create and maintain a balance among a family system.

The Family System

In general, here are some of the common roles that exist within a given family:

- Hero: the "good" or "responsible child."

- Rescuer: the one who takes care of the others' needs and emotions and acts at the problem solver for the family.

- Mediator: like the rescuer, but someone who acts as a buffer between different family members to avoid conflict.

- Scapegoat/Black sheep: the one the other family members think requires the most help (through therapy, rehabilitation, etc.) to succeed in life.

- Switchboard: the person in the family who is always in "the know" about other members' comings and goings.

- Power broker: the member of the family who enjoys being in control of the hierarchy of the family (and often with themselves at the top).

- Lost child: the child who is so quiet and obedient that he or she sometimes gets forgotten about.

- Clown: the person who uses humor to avoid conflict in the family.

- Cheerleader: the one who encourages and supports others.

- Nurturer: the person who provides comfort, emotional support, and safety for other members.

- Thinker: the family member who provides objective and reasoning focus.

- Truthteller: the person who you know will always tell you like it is.

  Please keep in mind that there can be multiple of each role in one family, and you may

even embody some of them. Further, sometimes they change depending on the situation you're in. For example, you are probably much more likely to speak your mind (being a truthteller) when you're around your immediate family, but you don't find it appropriate to readily offer your opinion (being more like a lost child) around your extended family.

It's also important to note that there are also different family types, including:

- Nuclear (aka elementary or traditional) – consists of two parents (usually married) and their biological or adopted children.

- Single Parent – consists of one parent and his or her children. In this situation, the parent was either never married, divorced, or widowed.

- Extended – consists of two or more adults who are related through blood or marriage with children who also live under the same roof as aunts, uncles, cousins, grandparents, and other relatives.

- Childless – consists of two partners who cannot have or don't want to have children.

- Stepfamily – consists of two families merging into one.

- Grandparent – consists of one or more grandparent who is raising their grandchildren because their children (the grandchildren's parents) are unable or incapable to.

- Kinfolk – consists of one or more friends who choose to live together (or at least close by) and possibly raise their families together.

Individual Needs vs. Family Expectations

One of the hardest parts about being heavily involved in a family is knowing when it's right to put your own needs over your family's expectations. This is especially tricky when it comes to things such as sports, hobbies, and beliefs. For instance, let's say your father and your older brothers were really good at football when they were your age. Well, you may feel a pressure to follow in their footsteps and play football.

But if that's not something you genuinely enjoy doing, you shouldn't do it. However, the idea of standing up to these often-unspoken expectations can be tricky. So, here are a few things to consider before bringing up your objections to your family (and we'll stick with the football example for analysis):

- **Identify unrealistic expectations.** Perhaps you're already in a sport that conflicts with football practices or games. Having that be the starting point (and then moving into the fact that you simply don't like playing football) can help alleviate the initial pressure off of you during the conversation.

- **Communicate openly and honestly.** Once you've discussed the unrealistic expectations, you can move into talking about your boundaries and goals. For example, maybe your goal is to make the varsity soccer next year. Well, you're not as likely to get there if you don't continue playing on the JV team this year.

- **Practice self-care.** Especially if your family is unhappy with your goal or boundary, it's important to continually reassure yourself that you're doing the right thing for you (despite how they may feel about it). Furthermore, as you work toward achieving a goal, you should be careful to eat a healthy diet, get plenty of sleep, relax when needed, and exercise regularly—as all of these activities will aid you in accomplishing it.

- **Seek professional help.** If the thought of speaking freely with your family feels daunting—or if your family didn't take what you said particularly well—perhaps you will benefit from talking things through with a professional therapist.

Changing Roles Over Time

As mentioned earlier, the roles you and other members of your family fill may change overtime—due to internal or external factors, such as traumatic shared or individual experiences, a chronic illness, a death, a divorce, a marriage, an injury, a birth, or career changes.

Moreover, roles have changed throughout history as time. Consider the following (according to the Pew Social Trends research):

- In the United States and in the year 1960, almost seventy-five percent of children lived with parents who were only married once and to each other. In 2014, that percentage dropped to under fifty percent.

- Also in 2014, fifteen percent of parents were re-married, seven percent were unmarried and cohabitating parents, twenty-six percent of children lived with single parents, and sixteen percent of children lived in a blended family (involving stepchildren, stepparents, and/or half-siblings).

- In 2017, there were over one million married, same-sex couples, and out of those people under fifty years old, forty-eight percent of women and twenty percent of men who identified as being a part of the LGBTQ+ community also reported raising children.

- Today, sixty-two percent of married partners (regardless of gender) agree that both partners work and share childcare and household responsibilities.

- As of 2012, twenty-seven percent of women have higher levels of education compared to their male spouses.

All of these changes in society have affected the way in which families function. Not many people exist as *Leave it to Beaver* would suggest. If you're unfamiliar, that was a black and white show back in the day that showed a traditional family in which the mother, June Cleaver, got all dolled up every single day just to stay at home and always had a hearty meal waiting for her husband when he came home from work.

Today, not all couples look like that or can effectively function (economically, emotionally, etc.) that way. And as time goes by, evolving societal norms will likely cause even more differences in family roles.

Contributing to Family Life

Regardless of your role(s) in your family, as you get older, you're going to be expected to contribute to your family members in ways you weren't responsible for as a younger kid. For instance, you may be required to offer a listening ear, empathy, and comfort to your family members in times of joy, stress, and everything in between.

Moreover, you should also prepare yourself for the future when you're going to need to provide financial stability, quality time, and other support to a family of your own.

4.2 COMMUNICATING WITH PARENTS AND OLDER SIBLINGS: BRIDGING THE GAP

As you get older, you'll probably find your parents and older siblings start talking to you more like an adult and less like a kid. However, that means that you need to learn how to effectively communicate with them.

Understanding Generational Differences

Generations refer to groups of people who were born and raised around the same time.

The current generations are as follows*:

- Traditionalists or Silent Generation: people born between 1925-1945
- Baby Boomers: people born between 1946-1964.

- Generation X: 1965-1979

- Millennials (Generation Y): 1980-1994

- Generation Z: 1995-2009

- Alpha: 2010 - ?

    Each generation comes with different values, beliefs, and sensibilities due to societal norms at the time and historical events that occurred when they were children.

For example, Baby Boomers were born and raised after WWII, meaning that they saw younger marriages higher birth rates, and a great scarcity of resources. In general, this led to members of that generation functioning under a mentality of "work as hard as you can."

Whereas Generation Xers were raised in a time that was characterized with early technological developments, transformative socio-political change (such as the Civil Rights Movement, the conclusion of the Space Race, and the Vietnam War), and minimal adult supervision. As a result, members of that generation tend to favor a work-play balance.

Then, as the name suggests, Millennials were born and raised around the turn of the century, and they were the last generation to experience life before technology completely took over our lives. In addition to seeing a major shift into the technological age, they were also old enough to witness and understand the tragic events of 9/11.

Moreover, they were mostly raised by Gen X parents, so they benefited from their prioritization of a work-life balance. Their childhood environments tended to produce progressive and empathetic adults who often try to incorporate morals into all aspects of their lives.

Last, but not least, (Alphas are perhaps too young to truly examine and understand yet), Generation Zers, aka "the first global generation," grew up in the emergence of social media apps, so they may not fully comprehend what it was like not to have just about the whole world (information and the ability to communicate with people around the globe) at your fingertips. However, similarly to the Baby Boomers, members of this generation tend to be hard working because they experienced the global financial crisis that happened between 2007 to 2009, and the COVID-19 pandemic. But they differ from Boomers in that they often feel comfortable expressing their thoughts, feelings, emotions, and opinions with others.

Understanding the framework from which adults around you are working from helps you communicate effectively and empathize with them.

* These are general years, some sources report different birth years, give or take a few.

Effective Communication Strategies

Speaking of effective communication, it's important for you as you get closer to adulthood to know how to talk with people—especially those who are older or hold authority over you.

Here are strategies to consider before having a conversation with someone:

1. **Convey important points clearly and concisely.** You'll be hard pressed to garner respect from someone by using too many filler words like "Um, uh, etc." And that's because they make you seem uncertain of yourself and the point you're trying to make. Instead, try to use as many action verbs (i.e., programmed, evaluated, examined, grew, arranged, advised) as you can, offer tangible and concrete terms, and end with a clear call to action if the conversation requires the person you're speaking with to do something.

2. **Be mindful of other modes of communication.** When you speak to someone face-to-face, be aware of the body language you're using to communicate with as well as your actual words. For example, Further, that same gesture may be seen as disrespectful to a parent who is trying to provide you with constructive criticism.

3. **Watch your tone.** Similar to your body language, the tone in which you speak also says a lot in addition to the words that are

actually coming out of your mouth. In general, your tone should match the message you're hoping to convey. Say you're hoping to get a later curfew, approaching that conversation in a jokey tone might convey that you aren't serious or mature enough to stay out later.

4. **Maintain your emotions.** This one isn't always easy, especially if the communication is particularly emotional. But similar to the last two points, you should be careful to match your emotion to the setting and situation you're in. For instance, you're not likely to get far when talking with your parents for more allowance if you're crying about your lack of money. Nobody likes witnessing desperation, and it makes you look more like a child than a young adult.

5. **Know your audience.** Before speaking with someone, try to get an understanding about how they think, feel, and operate as much as possible. This will help you understand how best to communicate with them.

6. **Engage in active listening**. You're much more likely to get a receptive audience if you give them and their voice respect in return. One of the best ways to do this is by simply closing your mouth and avoiding defensiveness and interruption. Then, when they're finished, try to give appropriate feedback, ask questions, or offer suggestions. If you're unsure of how to respond, there's no harm in asking for some time to mull things over.

7. **Request feedback.** In order to get better at communicating effectively, you should not be afraid to ask your parents, siblings, etc., for feedback on your approach. However, after asking for such criticism, please be as open and receptive as you can be without letting your pride get in the way.

I focused on verbal communication in this list, but most, if not all, of the points work forwritten and visual communications as well.

Building Mutual Respect

As you may have already started to realize, as you get older, the respect you get from and give to others, especially those in your family, is really important. Why? Because respect communicates trust, safety, and well-being for all parties involved.

But respect isn't something you should get or give naturally. Instead, it has to be earned. Below are five things to think about when hoping to gain or give respect:

1. **Lead by example.** Those who lead by showing kindness, grace, and compassion to others are often more respectable than those who do not. Further, look around and note the people in your life that you see being kind to and empathizing with others.

2. **Actively listen to others.** This demonstrates your respect for the other person, and it will likely result in them respecting you as well.

3. **Show appreciation and celebrate the achievements of others.** By affirming someone else's value, you are increasing the respect they have for the goals you accomplish.

4. **Avoid unconstructive criticism.** When you're hoping to change someone's behavior (let's say it's a sibling who you share a room with, and you want them to be tidier. You'll be much more successful if you start out with something positive (like how much you admire their studious nature, for instance) and then go into their shortcomings. Once they hear something positive about themselves, they'll be much more inclined to also listen to your constructive criticism.

5. **Take the time to get to know people.** You can't give or get respect without knowing those around you. This means taking the time, even with those you live with, to discuss each other's desires, goals, dislikes, interests, etc. Then, once you know more about someone, it's easier to empathize, understand, and relate to them. They'll likely feel the same about you.

Dealing with Disagreements

If you spend a significant amount of time with anyone, chances are that you're going to have a disagreement or two. It's just human nature—and disagreeing with someone doesn't always have to be seen as a negative thing. Instead, if done with respect, it can be a learning opportunity for all people involved.

Here are tips for managing conflict with family members:

- **Agree to negotiate.** First, decide if the issue is actually worth fighting over. Next, try to separate the problem from the person, cool off before talking if you feel too angry to speak calmly, and keep in mind that the goal is to resolve and not "win" in an argument. If in the end, you can't fully resolve something, you can always simply agree to disagree and go along your way.

- **Work as a team.** You must first both be willing to compromise, but once you are, you can work together to come up with as many possible solutions as possible, then narrow down to the best solution (as decided upon by both of you), and then do your best to stick to it.

- **Seek professional advice.** If you feel like you and your family members could benefit from advice from a neutral third party you can consider going to a doctor, therapist, or family counselor for help.

4.3 HANDLING SIBLING RIVALRY: FROM CONFLICT TO COOPERATION

Other than your parents, the first people you likely had conflict with (i.e., fought with) were your siblings. But although you may get scolded for it, it actually isn't all bad and actually has a psychological purpose. We'll dive deeper into all of that in this section.

Root Causes of Sibling Rivalry

As I just mentioned, researchers believe that sibling conflict and rivalry serves a psychological and developmental purpose, which is to help each person learn how to differentiate (uncover aspects of their personalities) that make unique.

Through disagreement and effective resolution, we learn what our skills and talents are. Plus, we also get a better understanding about our opinions and preferences.

We as people are also hard wired for social comparison. So, since our siblings are often around us and available for comparisons, they are often targeted.

Fair Play

Despite the positive outcomes of sibling rivalry, that doesn't mean the actual conflict itself isn't incredibly frustrating at times.

If you're like most, you've probably found yourself saying or thinking, "That's not fair!" Perhaps the inciting situation had to do with your brother or sister being allowed to stay out with their friends later than you. Or maybe on a particular night, they are allowed to bring friends over, but you are not.

The feelings and emotions you felt when a situation like those mentioned above occur are totally valid, and it's normal for them to be difficult to manage at times. However, what you should always be asking yourself is if there's a lesson you can learn from them. For example, let's return to the example about your sibling being able to stay out later than you.

The first step may be for you to feel upset and maybe even betrayed by your parents for not giving you the same curfew.

Again, that's perfectly valid. However, you must then also take a step back and analyze *why* those privileges are being afforded to your sibling and not you. Are they older than you? Many parents give later curfews depending on age. If not, or maybe in addition to, are they a better student than you? Proving to your parents that you are a responsible person will likely result in them trusting you more

. . . and later curfews and more liberties in general often come with that trust.

However, if you truly feel like your parents are treating you unfairly, don't hesitate to reach out to a guidance counselor, therapist, or other trusted adult for help. They will hopefully assist in analyzing the situation for you and finding solutions, if available and applicable.

Turning Rivalry into Teamwork

Another awesome part of becoming older is the realization that your siblings don't have to be your adversaries. Instead, they can actually be your teammates. Think about it. No matter how crazy they may make you feel sometimes, you else would you rather go to bat for? Chances are it's your family.

Hopefully they feel the same way, and the next time one of you is facing a challenge, try and discover how you can tackle it together.

This is not to say you should treat the world like a battlefield. But using your words to settle disagreements or stick up for your sibling is often even more powerful than using your fists.

Of course, this can also mean just simply being there for a sibling and being their cheerleader—in good and bad times. This will require both of you to accept and appreciate each other's individuality and differences.

Moreover, your siblings are probably some of the people in the world who know you best. They've likely experienced a lot of the same things as you, so they understand you (and vice versa) in ways others can't or won't—and that's incredibly valuable! Please be cautious in discarding that if you're lucky enough to have it.

4.4 APPRECIATING FAMILY VALUES: TRADITION MEETS THE MODERN WORLD

It may seem corny or cliché, but family is one of the greatest gifts we are given in this life. They are the people who often have our backs, teach us lessons, and are available and willing to lend us their ears.

You may have taken this for granted when you were younger, but you'd be cautioned to continue doing so as you get older. For one thing, during this time, you're likely going to experience and witness people around you who don't have the same support that you do. So, you'd be disserving God, the universe, or whatever else you believe in by failing to appreciate the gift and your luck for having it in the first place.

The Importance of Tradition

A key part in feeling part of your family is by participating in familial traditions, which may involve activities, gifts, stories, songs, etc., that *may* have been passed down from generation to generation.

However, traditions don't have to be some big thing that your great-grandparents used to do, for example. They may have just been established within the last few years or so. But in order to be considered a tradition, the activity (or whatever), has to be something you and others look forward to and feel closer to each other when participating in it.

For instance, some families watch specific movies and/or prepare special meals during the holiday season. Such things make us feel like we have a place in our families and in our culture.

Balancing Tradition and Individuality

But all of the above is not to say that you need to engage in your family's traditions if they go against who you are as a person, your morals, your beliefs, etc.

Let's suppose your family has a tradition of going out to hunt around the same time every year. Well, if that's not something you're interested in, you should not feel pressure to do so. However, please consider being as calm and kind when you first alert others to your disinterest. You should try not to shame members of your family who do enjoy the activity.

Remember what I said about accepting and appreciating each family member's individuality? That applies as long as no laws are being broken and nobody is getting hurt. If traditions involve those two results, then a bigger conversation needs to take place (and you would be advised to seek the help of a guidance counselor, therapist, etc. in that case).

Modernizing Traditions

Another unique position you're going to be put in as you get older is having the authority to suggest changes and updates to traditions. As our society moves forward, such modernization is often appropriate and for the better.

For example, I remember reading online about a family who had a tradition of giving each woman who was going to enter the family a "test." It involved things like cooking meals and other outdated and stereotypical things women use to be expected to do (and be good at) in the past.

Well, in that case, as long as the "test" was seen as something fun and silly (and not something that would <u>actually</u> bear weight on the relationship), a great way to bring that into this century would be to apply it to each person—regardless of age, gender, etc.—once a relationship or engagement has started. And of course, if anyone voices their opposition to participating, that should also be acceptable. Traditions shouldn't force people out of their free will.

As I touched on, such changes often need to be made in order to update traditional culture (in terms of religion, law, politics, social climates, etc.). But as with other things we've touched upon in this book, these revisions should be suggested in a calm and kind manner. If you start the conversation out on a sour or judgmental note, the less likely it will be that your "edits" to certain traditions will be received or even considered.

Creating New Traditions

Sometimes, you may discover traditions that your family's elders used to participate in that you'd like to see implemented today, or you may simply want to establish a completely new tradition.

In those situations, they're pretty easy to create—you simply have to do them. However, you need to first assess the feelings of others as to their openness and willingness to also participate. But as long as at least a few of you are interested . . . boom! You have a new family tradition.

4.5 CREATING YOUR SUPPORT SYSTEM: BEYOND BLOOD RELATIONS

We've focused exclusively on the traditional definition of family—meaning those that you are related to by blood, adoption, or relationship (i.e., those that your siblings, aunts, uncles, etc., are involved with romantically).

But fortunately, families are often made up of so much more, including friends, birth families of adopted children, pets, and anyone and anything in between.

Defining "Family"

In general, there are four ways in which sociologists (via the Burgess & Locke [1945] methodology) today use to define a family:

1. Structural.
2. Household-based.
3. Role-based.
4. Interactionist.

STRUCTURAL

This is the most traditional way to define a family, and it affords for members of one being legally linked to each other—through blood, marriage, adoption, etc.

While that is all fine and good, it also discredits a lot of other legitimate people involved in a family—such as long-time cohabitating couples, for example, who are not married. Under the law, especially in terms of insurance, the ability to make health decisions, trusts and estates, and more, such people are not seen equally as those who are married. Another example would be foster children. They do not have the same rights as blood or adopted children.

Basically, in order to structurally define a family, you have to consider who "real" members are. Often, this involves a contract, which a birth certificate, marriage license, adoption agreement, etc., can be considered in a court of law.

HOUSEHOLD-BASED

Quite simply, this approach considers whoever you share a living space* with to be your family. This is broader than the structural concept in that it includes cohabitating couples, friends, etc. But it's also narrower in that it excludes others who you don't actually live with. Moreover, some people live alone—and for most, it's unfair and untrue to say they don't have any family.

* Children of divorced or separated parents who have joint custody of them are considered family members under this definition in both households.

ROLE-BASED

This one examines someone's role in the family in order to dictate their place in a family—for example, a husband and a wife, a brother and a sister, a mother and a daughter, etc. The limits to this definition, of course, focuses on gender differentiations, the nuclear family, and heterosexuality.

In reality, people can exist independently of these traditional roles. Further, people don't need to be a husband, wife, sister, aunt, uncle, etc., to have a family.

INTERACTIONIST

This is the broadest approach, and it considers family in terms of the people who you communicate and create and maintain a culture with. According to Christopher Carrington, this means those who you engage in consistent and reciprocal patterns of loving and caring.

However, this is also limiting in that it doesn't include people who you may consider family but don't often interact with.

Building a Chosen Family

Chosen families are people we meet throughout our lives that we grow so close with that we start to consider them family, regardless of shared blood or legal obligation to.

For example, I consider the woman who babysat me from the time I was an infant to when I was old enough to stay home alone to be a part of my family. She's invited to every major event in my life, and we even say "I love you" to each other. In a similar vein, the best friend I've had since I was fourteen and his child are also my family.

The difference between the people I mentioned above and those who are in my family of origin is that we all chose—and continue to choose—to be family. That comes with dedication, trust, and support. Often, these bonds with our chosen family take time to develop and rarely just occur overnight (although they certainly can).

The Importance of Support Networks

Regardless of who you consider to be part of your family, the reason why you need these people in your life is because they encourage you, pick you up when you're down, and help you achieve all of your goals (personal, academic, financial, etc.). Not many can succeed alone and without a strong support network.

Maintaining Connections

The level of connection you hold with someone (again in terms of family of origin or chosen family) has to do with several factors—including your individual relationship with them, both parties' current life situation, and more.

For example, let's go back to my best friend from middle school. As you likely do with many of your friends, we used to be in the same school together and see each other every single day. Well, that changed when we both went to different colleges.

Today, as full-grown adults, we're still very important to each other, but we live about two hours apart. So, we both make conscious efforts to reach out and check in a few times a week. However, when he was a young father, I gave him extra space and the grace when he would take a few days to respond to my call or text. Similarly, he did the same for me when I was trying to establish myself in my career.

But for my ninety-seven-year-old grandmother, who didn't text or use Facebook Messenger, I would try my best to pop in and see her at her assisted living facility whenever I was home—and that continued when she was no longer as coherent or responsive as she once was. The important thing was just being there.

With each person in your life, take some time to analyze and assess how much capacity and space you have (and want) to dedicate to them. And in turn, how much you want them to afford to you. If you feel like there's an imbalance on either side, you should communicate that.

4.6 SUMMARY

At the end of the day, family is important. Hopefully you've already discovered this for yourself, or this book is helping you to understand that. But family dynamics do not come without their challenges—however, even through disagreements or times when you just simply seem to drift apart, try to love on your family members as much as you can.

We so often take them for granted. And something else you'll need to start realizing or wrapping your head around (if you haven't already) is that you truly never know how much time you have with someone on this earth. Remember, tomorrow is never promised for you or anyone else.

CHAPTER FIVE:
SUCCEEDING IN SCHOOL

Although you may not realize it yet, your success in school, especially during this point in your life and going forward, is so much more than getting "A's," getting into college someday, and succeeding in a career. Instead, it's also important in developing your self-esteem, decreasing your levels of depression and anxiety, and keeping you away from drug and alcohol abuse.

5.1 MASTERING TIME MANAGEMENT: BALANCING SCHOOL AND LIFE

Of course, there's also more in your life than school and homework. But the key is in effectively and accurately managing your time. This will help you achieve your goals while also help you stay as stress-free as possible.

Prioritization is Key

When it comes to balancing your life, in terms of schoolwork, extracurricular activities, time spent with friends and family, and more, the key is prioritization. This means actually listing them out on paper or simply in your mind in order from most important to least. Now, deeming something less pressing than another task does not mean you're saying it isn't paramount or special for you. Instead, you need to consider what things you need to accomplish in order to achieve your goals.

For instance, hopefully you've realized, or are starting to realize, that your academic success is going to set you up for a lifetime—academically, professionally, and personally. So, in most cases, your homework should be at the top of your to-do list. However, you may also have chores that you are responsible for, so those should probably be at a close second. Next, any time you've committed to practicing or attending games, competitions, etc., should also be high up on your priorities.

Then, any time you have left can be dedicated to time with friends, family, or self-care.

Creating a Schedule

One of the best ways for you to organize your time is by creating a schedule or calendar. You can use your phone or get a physical planner from the store.

Then, you may want to take time every week, say every Sunday night, for example, or at the start of every month, and chart how each day is going to look. Of course, you don't have to put down exact time frames, but you can if that helps you.

Just make sure you have reasonable expectations, deadlines, etc., mapped out. This will help you feel less stressed and more prepared to tackle your time and expectations.

Avoiding Procrastination

Perhaps the greatest culprit when it comes to stress and overwhelm is procrastination—meaning, the action of delaying or postponing something. Instead, tackling things head on and in a timely manner is the best way to live your life.

This is especially important when it comes to homework, projects, and studying because starting early and giving yourself as much time as possible to work, complete, and learn them will give you the best chance at creating an accurate, quality product to turn in or acing a test.

Adopting an "If not, when?" mentality is a great way for you to start each day and task. And, furthermore, I promise you'll thank yourself for work you do now when it comes to the future.

Tools for Time Management

Aside from everything we've already mentioned, here are a few more tips for managing your time:

1. **Know yourself.** Consider what time of day you feel most focused and alert. Whether that's right away in the morning, after lunch, in the evening, etc., try to schedule more brain-focused—such as studying, working on homework, and reading—for those times whenever possible. Further, you should also try to think about how long you tend to stay focused on one thing at a time and removing distractions.

2. **Accept that your life is a work in progress.** You aren't always going to get your schedule right every time. But that's okay. Move forward with the intention to do better next time.

3. **Consider things that are urgent.** When something is due or needs to be done in a short amount of time, we often tend to become stressed about accomplishing it. So, try your best to put the things that need to be done right away in order to avoid a major problem at the very top of your list.

4. **Try to identify time you "waste."** Let's say, for an example, that you scroll through social media for an hour before bed each night. Well, what if you cut that time in half and used the other thirty minutes to study for a big test you have coming up? Little changes like this help you manage you're your time effectively.

5.2 EFFECTIVE STUDY TECHNIQUES: BEYOND CRAMMING

Like we discussed above, delegating plenty of time to study for tests is the best way for you to feel prepared when it comes to actually taking one. In this section, we'll cover some different strategies for you to consider.

Active Learning Strategies

An active learning strategy is any activity that engages you in deep thought about the subject matter on a course you're currently taking.

This is the opposite of passive learning which occurs when you're sitting in class and learning about requirements of your homework or a project.

Instead, active learning requires for you to participate in your own learning.

Examples of active learning include:

- Clustering in small groups to discuss a topic.

- Reflecting individually at the end of each class about what you learned and what questions you might have for the next session.

- Working through an application problem with a partner before presenting it to a larger class.

- Asking questions in class, to a team, or on discussion boards.

Study or Work Environment

Before studying or working, please be considerate of different things that may help you feel more relaxed, productive, and focused. Including:

- **Privacy.** Creating a distraction-free zone is one of the best ways to ensure of your productivity. This sometimes means also turning off your phone or putting it on airplane mode. Of course, you shouldn't do this if you're expecting an important call.

- **Lighting.** Humans love natural light, so try to find a space that incorporates plenty of it as you work to keep focus and stay motivated.

- **Comfort.** This might go without saying, but like natural light, humans also adore comfort. However, this does not necessarily mean sitting with your back against a couch. Instead, you may want to find a chair that offers support to your back and your posture.

- **Noise.** Some find their favorite music is the best thing to put on right before studying or working. However, if you find that you're focusing more on the lyrics than on the task at hand, you may want to try instead listening to instrumental music or ambient noise. Further, you can try looking up particular playlists for focusing on YouTube, Spotify, etc.

- **Scents.** Essential oils, like lavender, rosemary, and peppermint, have been proven to increase concentration and retention of information. So, dabbing a little on your wrists before a study or reading session may help you in both areas.

- **Organization.** Unless you're one of the rare people who thrive on clutter, you probably want to make your study space as organized and clean as possible. This removes distractions and helps you stay focused. Here are a few tips:

    o Keep only the things you use every day within in reach (and store everything else off of your desk).

    o Hide supplies, tools, and clutter behind your monitor or under your desk.

- **Time.** Of course, as suggested already, you should carve out time in your day for things such as schoolwork and studying, but actually staring at a clock or timer while doing so may cause a sense of urgency and then act as a distraction.

- **Breaks.** Taking small and intentional breaks is a great way to reset and maintain endurance. Plus, especially if you're working on a computer, they aid in helping to avoid eye strain.

- **Your personality.** In general, we are most productive in places that we enjoy being in. So, be careful to decorate your study space with colors and décor that you like. Moreover, you may also find it beneficial to display some of the certificates and accolades you've acquired over the years around. Such things can boost your self-esteem.

Memory Aids

Sure, some people can read a sentence in a book or on a website and remember it. However, many of our minds don't work that way . . . and that's okay! Instead, we benefit from aids to help us remember information.

Here are five techniques for you to try out:

1. **Write, don't type.** Yes, we have technology today that helps us dictate notes faster than ever. But writing them down instead,

and in our own words, helps us remember them because our brain is processing them deeper.

2. **Visual aids.** Humans are visual people, so learning in a way that is visually satisfying and helps us analyze otherwise complex thoughts or ideas is a great way for us to learn and retain information. For example, mind maps, which allow you to create and understand the connections between certain types of information, are great for people your age.

3. **Read it aloud.** Just like when we write something in our own words, actually reading something out loud, especially without looking at the page or flashcard, helps us recall the information better.

4. Give yourself time. One of the best pieces of advice when it comes to memorizing information is to start learning it early and then repeat, repeat, repeat. Cramming will likely get you nowhere because it doesn't give you the time to step away from the information and assess what areas you're having trouble with.

5. **Sleep.** The process our minds go under when we're asleep actually help us form memories. For example, our long-term memories are formed while we're asleep. Thus, you learn the topics you've studied in a given day while you sleep that night.

The Pomodoro Technique

Pomodoro is the Italian word for tomato, and The *Pomodoro* Technique requires you to think in terms of tomatoes and not hours. This may sound incredibly silly, but a lot of people swear by this time management method. Here is how it's done:

- Step 1: Get out your to-do list and pick a topic.

- Step 2: Set a twenty-five-minute (each interval of this is a "*pomodoro*") timer.

- Step 3: Work on your chosen task until the timer is up.

- Step 4: Take a five-minute break.

- Step 5: After completing four *pomodoros* (so, four twenty-five-minute timers), take a longer fifteen-to-thirty-minute break.

You see, this technique works because it replaces something stressful (like time management) and makes it more arbitrary. You see, procrastination doesn't usually boil down to laziness. It actually has more to do with the avoidance of negative feelings.

Go on, give it a try! Maybe it'll work for you too.

5.3 COPING WITH ACADEMIC PRESSURE: STRESS MANAGEMENT STRATEGIES

I'm not going to beat around the bush—school can be stressful. You're in all of these classes, and each one has its own daily, weekly, and monthly requirements of you. Of course, that would make anyone stressed out from time to time. But that's the way the real world works as well, and you'll be faced with the same deadlines, tests, etc., once you're a working adult.

So, learning how to deal with all of the pressure now will only help you going forward into high school, college, and beyond.

Recognizing Stress

The first thing we need to learn when it comes to stress is how to identify when we're feeling it. And the symptoms can be different for everybody—for some, it may include feeling worried, irritable, restless, and on edge, for others it may make your mind feel like it's blank and cause sleep problems, headaches, stomachaches, pain, etc.

Basically, any time you feel out of control of your life and/or not at ease, you're probably stressed about something.

Healthy Stress Relief

However, and this is an important thing to understand, none of what was mentioned above means that stress is *inherently* bad. On the contrary, good stress is called eustress, and it's the emotions we feel when we're excited.

When we experience eustress, our pulses usually quicken and our hormones surge, but we aren't actually under threat or experiencing fear.

And bursts of eustress, motivate us, focuses our energy, and enhances our performance.

Seeking Support

Especially when feeling bad stress—i.e., the kind of stress that makes you feel worn out, tired, hopeless, etc.—please do not hesitate for a moment to reach out to a friend, family member, or anyone else that you feel like you can trust when you're vulnerable. Talking things out with someone like this is cathartic, and more likely than not, they've experienced something similar and can give you suggestions and advice for eliminating the stress going forward.

Guidance counselors and therapists are also wonderful people to reach out to for guidance on stress release.

Balanced Lifestyle

In the end, your goal in maintaining stress is all about creating a life that is satisfying, maintainable, realistic, and supportive of all of your values. This is what balance looks like.

Of course, this does not mean that you will ever be rid of bad stress completely—that isn't realistic. Instead, you need to learn how to make it as minimal as you can while also adopting coping mechanisms, such as breath work, problem solving, etc., for dealing with it when it does pop up from time to time.

5.4 SETTING ACADEMIC GOALS: SHORT-TERM WINS AND LONG-TERM VISIONS

When it comes to setting your goals in school, it may be best to think of them in terms of short-term and long-term successes. The short-term ones are relatively done with less effort and require less time than the more long-term visions you may have. However, that doesn't mean either of them are more important than the other.

SMART Goals

SMART goals help you clearly define and meet your objectives. It's an acronym for Specific, Measurable, Achievable, Relevant, and Time-Bound.

Here is what to consider when writing SMART goals:

- **S: Specific**—What needs to be accomplished? What steps need to be taken in order for it to be accomplished?

- **M: Measurable**—How much time do you need in order to achieve your goal?

- **A: Achievable**—Is your goal actually achievable in the amount of time you've decided?

- **R: Relevant**—Why are you setting the goal you're setting?

- **T: Time-Bound**—What's your time horizon? When will you consider your goal "accomplished?"

An example of a SMART-goal statement might be: My goal is to [quantifiable objective] by [timeframe or deadline]. I will accomplish this goal by [what steps you'll take to achieve the goal]. Accomplishing this goal will [result or benefit].

SMART goals can be established for both short and long-term accomplishments you hope to make in your life.

Breaking Down Goals

If you don't like the SMART goal strategy, or have a particularly big goal to achieve, here's another process you can try:

- **Step 1: Define the outcome of your goal.** When working to achieve something, you want to make sure that your efforts are actually bringing you closer to that specific goal.

- **Step 2: Outline to goals process.** No matter what you're hoping to achieve, you're likely going to need to take different but calculated steps to do so. For instance, let's say you want to get ace a class. In order to do that, you'll need to pay attention while the teacher is lecturing, do well on all of your homework, work hard on all projects, and set up and stick to a study schedule for each test.

- **Step 3: Map out the projects.** Let's stick to the goal of acing a class. Well, as we said, you're going to have certain "steppingstones"—homework, projects, tests, etc.—that you will need to complete along the way in order to achieve that over-arching goal. And for each one, it may help you to map out exactly what you need to do (like milestones) in order to succeed on each one.

Please be cautioned that sometimes breaking down your goals can make you start feeling overwhelmed or worried about achieving them. That's perfectly normal and actually your brain's way of protecting you. Just try to brush passed it the best you can and take everything a day and a task at a time.

If you feel like you need additional help, ask a friend or parent to be your "coach," meaning that they will do their best to hold you accountable to the actions and goals you've outlined.

Tracking Progress

If you're anything like me, then you love a good to-do list because you crave and get satisfaction out of the feeling of crossing an item off of it once you complete it. This is a way of tracking your success when working to accomplish a goal, and it can serve as motivation as you go forward.

However, you can track your success in many other ways, such as journaling about how far you've come or reflecting back on the SMART or other goal-mapping processes, for example.

The desired result here is just to keep you focused and striving for success by reflecting on what you've already accomplished.

5.5 EXPLORING EXTRACURRICULARS: BUILDING A WELL-ROUNDED PROFILE

As you head for our just start high school, you want to start thinking about your life after your senior year. And no matter what your goal for that time in your life is—whether it's to attend college, start a career, join the military, volunteer abroad, etc.—extracurricular activities help build you as a person and will help spruce up any application or resume. Why? Because they let people know more about you as a person and often communicate on your behalf that you know how to speak to people, and that you can work as a team to achieve a common goal.

Benefits of Extracurricular Activities

Some of these were already mentioned above, but they bear repeating. The benefits of extracurricular activities include:

- **Cultivating leadership opportunities.** Most sports or other activities you participate in out of your traditional schooling give you the opportunity to function in a leadership role. This helps you develop skills you will need, such as how to speak with someone from a place of authority, and benefit from in the future.

- **Enhancing the teamwork experience.** Whether playing a sport, performing in a play, participating in a club, etc., you will need to work with your peers in some capacity. Quickly, by doing this, you will likely learn how every single person on this planet comes with different experiences and outlooks on this in life, and learning how to work with people from all walks of life is important.

- **Developing time management skills.** Middle school and high school are both pretty busy times for students, and if you take on extra curriculars outside of the already hustling and bustling academic responsibilities you have, you are demonstrating even more competence in managing your time—which is a skill that will apply and help you in many areas of life (including looking good on a college application, for instance).

- **Promotes networking skills.** In the professional world, being able to strike up a conversation with your peers and others in similar fields as you are important ways to climb your way to success. Participating in an extra-curricular activities can give you the tools to do that in the future by forcing you to speak, make compromises with, and just work with other people.

- **Fosters confidence.** Just like with anything else, when you succeed in something (and especially something you enjoy doing) makes you feel good about yourself . . . and who doesn't want to feel like that from time to time?

- **Increases academic performance.** Extra curriculars promote passion, focus, and concentration. So, once you learn and establish these on the football field, for example, you can easily transfer them into the classroom.

Finding Your Interests

Again, we are all individual people, and that means that we all take interests in different things. The important work you have to do is finding the *right* extracurriculars for you—and remember, they have to be something that you genuinely enjoy doing. Otherwise, you're just wasting your time and everyone else's around you.

If you're unsure of what offerings your school and community have, please consider scheduling an appointment with your guidance counselor or calling your local rec center. But in general, here are common activities you can participate in:

- **Clubs**—whether designated by school topic (math, English, history, science, etc.), hobbies (film, music, art, drama, trivia, robotics, writing, poetry, etc.), a language, a civil rights cause (animal rights, Amensty International, Gay-Straight Alliance, etc.), or really anything else, there's probably a club out there for you to join and bond with peers over common interests.

- **Sports**—anything from the more traditional sport, like baseball, soccer, football, cheerleading, swimming, etc., to the imaginative Quidditch club can be a great way for you to bond with people similar to you while also getting in exercise.

- **Academic competitive teams**—there are certain mathematics, forensics, poetry, technology, robotics, and many other kinds of teams you can join and compete on behalf of.

- **Community programs**—Habitat for Humanity, 4-H, Key Club, and Kids Helping Kids, are all examples of programs you can volunteer or otherwise become a part of.

- **Government**—joining a community youth board, running for your school's student council, and participating in youth government are all ways to get involved with your peers and your community.

- **Military**—you can look into joining the Junior ROTC or Civil Air Patrol.

- **Other**—if you're interested in something, the chances are that there is a club, program, or something else that you can join. But if you find that there somehow isn't, you can always consider starting one of your own!

Balancing Academics and Extracurriculars

Finding the perfect (and healthy) balance between your schoolwork and extra-curricular activities might seem impossible sometimes, but I promise that it isn't.

First, you need to prioritize your academics. No matter what, these come first—and to prove that, most activities, especially sports, require you to maintain a certain GPA in order to participate in them in the first place. So, if you're struggling in a class, please reach out to your teachers and consider getting a tutor.

Second, you should be careful to choose activities that are important to you and not just because you think they'll make you look good to your peers or on a college application. If you aren't passionate about something, you likely aren't going to take it seriously or set aside the necessary time for it. Moreover, you don't want to take on too many extra-curricular activities.

Third, take necessary breaks for some down time and relaxation. Many make the mistake of overworking themselves, and that's how burnout and other negative outcomes start to happen. Your sleep, meditations, and any other form of self-care need to be scheduled into your everyday mix as well.

5.6 SUMMARY

During this time of your life, school is one of the most important things that you need to focus on—but that doesn't mean that you can't and shouldn't make time for other things—such as extra-curricular activities and down-time by yourself or with your friends and family.

When it comes to your life remember that important seven-letter word: B-A-L-A-N-C-E. We all need it to survive and succeed.

CHAPTER SIX:
CAREER EXPLORATION AND GOAL SETTING

We've hinted at your future career in earlier chapters, but in this one, we're going to take a deep dive into the subject.

Although you may think you have a long time to decide what you want to do in order to support yourself as an adult, in reality, you really don't. And deciding at least a few areas you might want to consider working in will help you decipher and make goals.

6.1 DREAM BIG: UNCOVER YOUR PASSIONS AND TALENTS

You've probably heard someone say, "As long as you do what you love, you'll never work a day in your life?" Well, I can tell you that's one-hundred percent true. So, when picking a career, you should rely on your natural talents and your interests.

For example, if you hate math, statistics, and financial theory, you probably aren't going to succeed as an actuary—someone who analyzes the financial costs or risk and uncertainty. Further, you probably wouldn't enjoy working in that position anyway.

However, if you have a passion for horses, let's say, perhaps becoming a trainer or a veterinarian is more up your alley.

Self-Assessment

Kind of like in our examples above, you just need to sit down and think about the things that you really enjoy doing, either while in school, in your free time, or both. Then, you'll want to investigate what type of careers incorporate those things.

The final step will be to either search or ask people who already work in those industries what their day-to-day activities look like. For instance, suppose the idea of being a pharmaceutical salesperson seems like something you might be interested in. However, after you learn that they have to travel around the country all of the time and give presentations to a bunch of people, you decide that isn't the right fit for you because you hate flying and public speaking.

Everything needs to be considered before you even begin the process of choosing a career path.

Exploring Passions

If you aren't sure which direction you might go into when it comes to your career, do not be afraid to experiment and explore your different passions. This is absolutely the time in your life where you're allowed and even encouraged to do so.

Have you always wanted to try out archery? Do it! What about skateboarding? Try it out. You never know what you might find and learn about yourself and your potential career along the way.

Vision Board Creation

Vision boards are collages you make using images found in magazines, online, or anywhere else, words, and imagery that speak to you and what you want to accomplish in life.

To get an idea, I made one in college after struggling in an astronomy class. In order to get myself motivated to go to class and study, I made a board covered with images of stars and words like "success", "intelligence" and "inspiration". When I was finished, I hung it on my desk and was forced to look at it multiple times a day.

Well, wouldn't you know it, the subject matter started becoming more interesting to me, and I got an "A" in the class.

This may seem like an incredibly simple concept, but I promise that it works. You know why? Because they are a visual reminder of your intentions. We've already talked about manifestation, and this is just another way to do it.

By combining the imagery of the galaxy and the words I wanted to see associated with it, I put my mindset in a place that strove for success in that class.

Inspiration from Role Models

Another great place to look at potential careers from is by observing your role models. Did a guidance counselor or teacher really help you out, and you'd love to do the same for someone one day? Well, that's a great starting place.

Of course, that doesn't mean you have to become a guidance counselor or a teacher, but what it tells you is that you have a desire to help people. And if that's the case, you're in luck because there are a lot of careers out there that aim to do exactly that.

6.2 GOAL SETTING: CREATING A ROADMAP FOR SUCCESS

Just like anything else in life, having a career requires you to make a map of actions and celebrate "little" wins along the way. For example, you can't just decide one day that you want to be a lawyer. It doesn't work that way. You have to get a high school diploma (of get a GED) and then a college degree, take the LSAT, which you have to take to get into law school, attend and graduate law school, and then pass a bar exam for the state you want to practice in.

Long-Term Vision

Given everything I just said, you often have to start with a long-term vision and work backwards from there. So, in the example I provided, the long-term goal is to become a lawyer.

However, please know that your ultimate goal can change and morph into something else as you go along.

Actionable Steps

As I demonstrated in the beginning of this section, once you've decided what the long-term goal is, you need to research and determine what steps you'll need to take in order to get there.

Let's move away from the lawyer example and instead consider that you want to become a police officer. Well, in order to do that (all states are different when it comes to these requirements, but just treat this list as hypothetical), you'll need a high school diploma or GED, have a relatively clean criminal record and a valid driver's license, and obtain a two-year associate degree within five years of employment.

Flexibility in Planning

I mentioned this before, but what's great about this stage in your life is that you can always change or edit your goals for the future. You aren't tied down to any college or career choice right now, so don't be afraid to play with several choices along the way.

Moreover, please also remember that not everyone's path to a similar ending is the same. For example, I changed my trajectory multiple times. When I was first applying for college, I wanted to be in health care. Then, I decided against that and enrolled in school as an English education major. Well, that changed when I decided art education might be more fun. However, I eventually graduated with degrees in journalism with a minor in sociology just to end up not working in either of those areas for a living. I'm telling you all of this to show you that everyone's story is different, and as long as you have good intentions and work hard, you'll end up right where you belong.

As you go along, just please take the time to sit down and review your goal and the steps you've taken so far to make sure that everything is still aligning with who you are and what you want out of life.

6.3 THE WORLD OF WORK: UNDERSTANDING DIFFERENT CAREERS

In order to determine which career might be the right one for you, you need to research every nook and cranny that you can about it. You need to know what the work generally entails, what the physically demands are of that work, what type of people you're going to be dealing with in connection with that work, and more. It probably isn't possible to know *too much* about a career before you start pursuing it.

Career Research

Aside from interviewing people who are in the industries and positions you hope to be in someday, you can also use the U.S. Bureau of Labor Statistic's Occupational Outlook Handbook (you can find it at bls.gov/ooh/) to find things like job summaries, the amount of entry-level education you need, the median pay for several different jobs, and more.

You can either search for an occupation or find them in different categories (such as industry or what letter they start with).

Informational Interviews

We've touched on this above, but here are a few questions you should consider asking in an interview with someone who works in a profession or industry you are interested in:

Generally Speaking

- Could you describe your typical workdays?

- What skills are required in your position on a day-to-day basis?

- What parts of your job do you find most challenging?

- What do you find most enjoyable about your job?

- What are the negative sides of your job?

- How many hours do you work in a typical week?

- Which seasons of the year are toughest in your job?

- Does your work involve any lifestyle changes, such as frequent travel or working on the weekends and on Holidays?

- Considering all of the people you've met in your field, what personal attributes are essential for success?

State of the Industry

- Do you think this field is growing enough so that there's room for someone like me?

- In your opinion, are too many or too few people entering this profession?

- What developments on the horizon could affect future opportunities?

- This industry has changed dramatically in the past five years. What have you seen from inside your company? Where do you think the changes will happen in the next five years?

- How frequently do layoffs occur? How does it affect employees' morale? Why do people leave this field or company?

- Who are the most important people in the industry today?

- Which companies have the best track record for promoting women and minorities?

- Are there opportunities for self-employment in your field? Where?

Money and Advancement Opportunities

- What would be a reasonable salary range to expect if I entered this field? What is the long-term potential?

- What is the advancement potential in the field? What is a typical path?

- How did you get your job?

- If you could start all over again, would you change your career path in any way? Why?

- How long does it take for managers to rise to the top?

- What is the background of most senior-level executives?

Skills, Experience, and Misc.

- What educational preparation would you recommend for someone who wants to advance in this field?

- What qualifications do you seek in a new hire?

- How do most people enter this profession?

- How does your company compare with others we've discussed?

- What professional organizations and journals should I be aware of?

- What else do you think I should know about your career?

    Please consider these as guidelines and feel free to add and erase as your conversation goes along. Further, you may want to consider talking to multiple people—both men and women in a given industry and in different positions to get a full idea of how a career in that field looks. In order to get the name and number of someone, you can additionally ask: Who else would you recommend I speak with? When I call, may I use your name?

Emerging Industries

You should feel free to go into whatever occupation you deem fit, but it is also important to consider what industries are emerging, which means there is a lot of growth potential in them . . . and that means opportunities (and money) for employees and investors.

For example, these industries are considered by most to be "emerging" as of now:

- Auto-generated intelligence.

- Information technology (IT).

- Solar power.

- 3-D printing.

- Advancements in healthcare.

- Hybrid and electric vehicles.

- Driverless cars.

- Cybersecurity.

- Renewable energy.

- Augmented reality.

- Infrastructure.

- Real estate.

This list might look a little different by the time you are ready to enter the workforce, but you get the idea for now.

If you want to participate in exciting, rapidly changing markets and advancements for the future, emerging industries might be of particular interest to you.

Workplace Skills

No matter what career you ultimately decide to pursue, there are certain skills you're going to need to acquire in a professional setting, including good communication, management, problem-solving abilities, organization, self-regulation, technical know-how, and an openness to learning and working with others as a team.

Here are four ways in which you can improve your workplace skills:

1. **Prioritize your daily tasks.** Give yourself a top list of tasks to try to finish every day. That way, you can monitor your progress and evaluate what you learned from the successes or failures at the end of the workday.

2. **Focus on one task at a time.** By focusing on one task alone, you are able to learn more about that specific task and gain more knowledge from the implementation of it.

3. **Set weekly and monthly milestones.** They can be a huge motivator and boost your self-confidence. If you need help deciding what these goals should be, ask your manager or boss to collaborate and brainstorm with you.

4. **Ask for feedback.** Asking your coworkers for regular honest and constructive criticism to you can also help you accomplish your milestones.

Moreover, below are three ways in which you can highlight your workplace skills when applying for a job:

1. **Select the skills applicable to the position you applied for.** Recruiters are typically looking for certain keywords or "buzzwords" when scanning resumes, and the job description itself should be a good place to look for which ones you might want to include in yours. Depending on the circumstance, you

may list your skills in a separate section of your resume but listing them as part of your competencies may help make them stand out.

2. **Align your skills with your job responsibilities.** Outline what you've done for previous employers such as: increased sales, improved efficiency, and reduced costs.

3. **Quantify your accomplishments**. Use specific metrics and statistics to prove what you can do. For instance, suppose your project management saved employees fifteen hours of work a month and increased productivity by ten percent.

Although it may seem silly to be reading about things you'll need to do when you're older, a lot of this can still be applied to you and your life now—in terms of running for student council, trying out to be elected as the capitan of your football team, just trying to be a good student, etc.

Now, more than ever, you need to learn how to not only conduct yourself in a respectful manner but also be open to criticism from others in order to become the best version of yourself.

6.4 NETWORKING 101: MAKING CONNECTIONS THAT COUNT

Networking is an important part of being a successful professional because it requires you to engage with others to learn about industry standards and job opportunities. But how exactly does networking work, and what does it entail? We'll cover all of that in this section.

Building a Professional Network

A professional network is a group of people who have built relationships with each other based on business experiences and similar interests and experiences. '

The following are examples of places where you can meet people to add to your network:

- Conventions.

- Business luncheons.

- Events within your current organization.

- On business-oriented social sites.

- Social events.

- Alumni association events.

- Trade shows.

- Fundraising events.

- Professional association events.

- Online courses for classes.

And the benefits of building a network include:

- Connecting with potential clients.

- Helping you identify opportunities for professional growth.

- Providing you with a group of experts in a particular field.

- Allowing you to gain knowledge and advice within your industry.

- Providing you with the opportunity to generate business referrals.

- Helping you stay on top of the latest trends within your field or industry.

- Offering you opportunities to gain professional mentors and contacts.

- Helping you learn about open positions in companies you may be interested in.

- Giving you the chance to take advantage of others' more expansive knowledge in a particular area.

The Importance of Mentors

A mentor is someone with knowledge and experience in your desired field who is willing to share his or her knowledge with you to help you achieve your goals. Ideally, your mentor will be someone who has achieved the level of success that you hope to achieve yourself *and* is willing to push you in ways others can't or won't.

Finding a mentor, or several, is important because it will provide you with immense benefits, such as the knowledge mentioned before, expanded networks, and chances to advance your career.

However, you need to be careful to find the right people because they need to be professionals who, after developing a relationship with you, are willing to stand in your corner, cheer you on, offer feedback, and support your growth personally and professionally.

Networking Etiquette

When networking, there are certain things you should keep in mind as far as etiquette and common courtesies go.

So, here are some of the dos and don'ts of networking:

- **Do:**

  - **Be authentic.** People can tell right away when you aren't being your genuine self, and that's a huge turn off.

  - **Listen more than you talk.** Remember that networking isn't only about you. It's about establishing relationships that are beneficial for all people involved. Plus, it's kind of pointless to network with someone whose opinions and knowledge you don't want to hear in the first place.

  - **Be professional.** Networking isn't like hanging out with your buddies in your basement. Instead, you need to present yourself in a professional manner by wearing appropriate attire, using proper grammar, and being respectful of others. Essentially, you want to paint yourself in the best light possible.

- **Don't:**

  - **Be too aggressive.** While you should be confident, you also need to be careful not to come on too strong. Nobody likes feeling pressured or pushed into things.

  - **Forget to follow up.** After meeting someone, make sure that you always send them an email or LinkedIn (we'll talk more about this website very soon) message to continue the conversation. Always thank them for their time speaking with you—this will show them that you're interested in establishing a professional relationship and that you value their time.

- o **Be negative.** Especially when first building a relationship with someone, it's important to avoid complaining or talking negatively about others when networking. On the contrary, you want to focus on positive topics and find common ground with the person you're talking to.

Leveraging Social Media

LinkedIn is a social media site that is just like Facebook, X (formerly known as Twitter), Instagram, and others in that you can add friends, make and comment on posts, and directly message people. The only difference is its main objective is to showcase your career and portfolio.

However, that doesn't mean you can't use the other sites mentioned to network—it can just be a little trickier because you may not have always been as professional on them as you need to be on LinkedIn.

While we're on the topic of social media, I will also caution you, as a general rule, to stop and think before you post *anything*—"Will this have an impact on me in five or ten years' time?" Meaning, will you want prospective bosses to see what you're about to post? If the answer is no, the best option is to delete it and move on.

Remember, once you click "post," that image or words you put out into the world will be there forever.

6.5 PREPARING FOR THE FUTURE: SKILLS FOR TOMORROW'S WORLD

As you age, you will only benefit from acquiring the skills that will make you an important and useful candidate in the professional world.

Future-Proofing Your Skills

For example, there is a platform called the World Economic Forum's Reskilling Revolutions, and it hopes to reach more than six million people by the year 2030 and prepare them for the global workforce by focusing on areas, such as energy renewal, artificial intelligence (AI), big data, and programming, *and* characteristics, such as leadership, curiosity, and resilience. It is believed that once an individual familiarizes themselves in all areas mentioned above, they will, in essence, future-proof their skills.

Other future-proof skills include being proactive, flexible, and ready for anything.

Once you have them, you are prepared for the future by developing a diverse and relevant set of competencies that will enable you to perform well in any situation.

Continuous Learning

Everything said in the previous section does not mean that you should not be encouraged from continually learning. Our world, especially when it comes to technology, is constantly changing and evolving, so if you want to be ahead of the curve, you'll want to have an ever-curious mind. In fact, depending on the career you choose, in general, if it requires you to have a license to actually do it, you'll likely be required to do a minimum of CLE (continued learning education) courses ever year or more.

Career Adaptability

As mentioned, industries are always changing, and that requires adaptability. So, it is imperative that you learn how to adapt to change in order to be a competent individual and employee. That may mean you have to learn and abide by new or changing laws, seamlessly transition into new or different positions or roles, and just roll with the punches that are thrown at you in a given day.

Innovation and Creativity

Innovation and creativity often involve the freedom to take risks while also being free from consequences of failure or punishment. So, if you chose a career that requires a lot of both or either—like a game developer, artist, novelist, scientist, etc.—please be careful to either establish this kind of environment or pick to work for a company that already does.

6.6 SUMMARY

Even though you may only be in middle school or just started high school, it is never too early for you to sit down and reflect on what you might want to do for a living in the future. For that decision, will have an impact on the kind of person you want to be and the goals you hope to achieve.

But that doesn't mean that you can't continually change your mind as you adopt new hobbies or dabble in different courses at school.

Again, as long as you're focus is on doing well in class and being a good, kind, and open person, you'll end up in the right place at the end of the day.

Dear reader:

Whew! All I have to say is, way to go, champ! You made it through the end of this book, and I, for one, am incredibly proud of you.

We've gone through a lot to get to this point. We have talked about your emotional intelligence, how to navigate your social relationships, planning your academic, professional, and personal future, mastering your practical life skills, digital literacy and safety, and how to prioritize your mental, physical, emotional, and mental health.

Trust me, I get it. None of the subjects above are for the faint of heart, but they are the trickier parts of life that need to be addressed, studied, and acted upon in order to be a successful young man in the future, which, I have no doubt that you will be now that you've stuck it out to the end of this book.

However, none of that means that your journey is anywhere from over, and I hope you'll circle back to this book time and time again if you need a quick refresher course on any of the material we discussed. Further, I hope you also feel inspired to go and seek out additional material on the subject of becoming a well-rounded young man.

Here is a list of my recommended reads:

- *Chop Wood Carry Water: How to Fall in Love with the Process of Becoming Great* by Joshua Medcalf.

    Amazon description: "Guided by "Akira-sensei," John comes to realize the greatest adversity on his journey will be the challenge of defeating the man in the mirror. This powerful story of one boy's journey to achieve his life long goal of becoming a samurai warrior, brings the Train to be Clutch curriculum to life in a powerful and memorable way."

- *Of Boys and Men: Why the Modern Male is Struggling, Why it Matters, and What To Do About It* by Richard V. Reeves.

    Amazon description: "Boys are falling behind at school and college because the educational system is structured in ways that put them at a disadvantage. Men are struggling in the labor market because of an economic shift away from traditionally male jobs. And fathers are dislocated because the cultural role of family provider has been hollowed out. The male malaise is not the result of a mass psychological breakdown, but of deep structural challenges.

    Structural challenges require structural solutions, and this is what Richard V. Reeves proposes in Of Boys and Men – starting boys at school a year later than girls; getting more men into caring professions; rethinking the role of fatherhood outside of a nuclear family context.

Feminism has done a huge amount of good in the world. We now need its corollary – a positive vision of masculinity that is compatible with gender equality."

- *The Mountain is You: Transforming Self-Sabotage Into Self-Mastery* by Briana Wiest.

  Amazon description: "This is a book about self-sabotage. Why we do it, when we do it, and how to stop doing it—for good. Coexisting but conflicting needs create self-sabotaging behaviors. This is why we resist efforts to change, often until they feel completely futile. But by extracting crucial insight from our most damaging habits, building emotional intelligence by better understanding our brains and bodies, releasing past experiences at a cellular level, and learning to act as our highest potential future selves, we can step out of our own way and into our potential. For centuries, the mountain has been used as a metaphor for the big challenges we face, especially ones that seem impossible to overcome. To scale our mountains, we actually have to do the deep internal work of excavating trauma, building resilience, and adjusting how we show up for the climb. In the end, it is not the mountain we master, but ourselves."

- *The Growth Mindset for Teens: Practical Lessons & Activities to Build Confidence, Problem Solve, Grow Skills, and Become Resilient in 31 Days* by Sydney Sheppard.

  From the Amazon description: "Turn your setbacks to breakthroughs and fears to power with this guidebook on developing a growth mindset — become a responsible and resilient adult!

You are no longer a child, but not yet an adult. As a teen, you are in a period in your life where more is expected of you as adulthood draws near.

You might find yourself overwhelmed by the pressure from your parents, teachers, and others around you.

What if I fail? What if I don't know how to be an adult? What if my parents are going to be disappointed in me? What if I don't land a lucrative career?

Suffocating what-ifs flood your mind, affecting your peace of mind which manifests in difficulties at school and challenges with relationships.

The truth is, you're not alone in this struggle. Millions of young people share the same dilemma, and even non-teens recognize the woes of emerging adulthood."

- *The Pivot Year* by Brianna Wiest.

  Amazon description: "This is the year you change your life. There's a saying that when the moment comes, you don't need words on a page, you need new thoughts in your head. When the moment really comes when you have to find your courage, when you have to let go, when you don't know what to do, you aren't going to go to your book shelf to try to find the answer. You need it with you here and now. Devote the next twelve months of your life to making measured and real change, beginning with your mindset. *The* Pivot *Year* is a book of 365 daily meditations on finding the courage to become who you've always wanted to be, from the internationally bestselling author of *101 Essays That Will Change The Way You Think, The Mountain Is You,* and more."

- *The 7 Habits of Highly Effective Teens* by Sean Covey.

  Amazon description: This card deck companion to Sean Covey's *The 7 Habits of Highly Effective Teens* is the essential go-to resource for busy teenagers preparing for a highly effective and successful life. Use the tools in these 52 cards to build the confidence you need to take on challenges, do hard things, and create lasting change.

Nevertheless, I just want to wish a heartfelt thank you to each and every one of you who read this book. It's my sincere wish that you got something out of it, and if you did, please pass it (and any other inspirational material you might stumble upon down the road) to your friends. There is always power in numbers, and we'll only be a better society when more young men have planned for their futures, come to terms with their emotions, and learned what it takes to be successful in this world.

I wish you all the best in your future endeavors, and I believe you were put on this earth to do great things . . . so get out there and do them!

Sincerely,

James Foster

"The good man is the man who, no matter how morally unworthy he has been, is moving to become better."

~John Dewey

REFERENCES

5 easy ways to boost your teenager's memory. (n.d.). https://parenting.etonhouse.edu.sg/5-easy-ways-to-boost-your-teenagers-memory#:~:text=2)%20Visual%20aids&text=This%20is%20why%20we%20use,and%20engage%20with%20the%20topic.

7 Tips for Empathic Listening | Crisis Prevention Institute (CPI). (n.d.). Crisis Prevention Institute (CPI). https://www.crisisprevention.com/blog/general/7-tips-for-empathic-listening/

7 steps to having positive online discussions. (n.d.). DoSomething.org. https://www.dosomething.org/us/articles/steps-positive-online-discussions

8 Ways You Can Improve Your Communication Skills - Professional & Executive Development | Harvard DCE. (2024, January 8). Professional & Executive Development | Harvard DCE. https://professional.dce.harvard.edu/blog/8-ways-you-can-improve-your-communication-skills/

12 tips to balance academics and extracurricular activities | The Princeton Review. (n.d.). https://www.princetonreview.com/college-advice/12-tips-to-balance-academics-and-extracurriculars

REFERENCES

40 questions to ask in an informational interview. (2021, September 27). School of Management - University at Buffalo. https://management.buffalo.edu/career-resource-center/students/networking/mentorlink/40-questions-to-ask-in-an-informational-interview.html

Active Learning Strategies - Active Learning - Purdue University. (n.d.). https://www.purdue.edu/activelearning/Need%20Help/alstrategies.php

Alexandrova, M. (2023, February 22). *Mutual respect: How to build it in your workplace.* TestGorilla. https://www.testgorilla.com/blog/mutual-respect/

Allinachill. (2022, July 1). *Life balance.* Change to Chill. https://www.changetochill.org/finding-balance/

American Lung Association. (n.d.). *Breathing exercises.* https://www.lung.org/lung-health-diseases/wellness/breathing-exercises

American Psychological Association. (2022, May). *Reslilience.* apa.org. https://www.apa.org/topics/resilience

Anxiety and stress in teens. (2023, December 20). Johns Hopkins Medicine. https://www.hopkinsmedicine.org/health/conditions-and-diseases/anxiety-disorders/anxiety-and-stress-in-teens#:~:text=Symptoms%20can%20include%20worries%2C%20feeling,%2C%20headaches%2C%20stomachaches%20and%20pain.

Applebury, G. (2023, May 3). *Common family roles and their evolution over time.* LoveToKnow. https://www.lovetoknow.com/life/relationships/common-family-roles-how-theyve-changed

Awa, E. (2023, October 27). *How to Future-Proof your skills and stay ahead of the curve.*

https://www.linkedin.com/pulse/how-future-proof-your-skills-stay-ahead-curve-echezonachi-awa-iyilf/

Bare Addiction. (2024, March 28). *The Best skincare Routine for Teen Boys: Comprehensive guide.* https://bareaddiction.com/blogs/blog/the-best-skincare-routine-for-teen-boys-a-comprehensive-guide-to-clear-healthy-skin

Barge, M. A. (n.d.). *Complete list of extracurricular activities: 100s of examples.* https://blog.prepscholar.com/list-of-extracurricular-activities-examples#google_vignette

Beckwith, R. (2024, April 19). *Batch cooking for beginners.* Good Food. https://www.bbcgoodfood.com/howto/guide/batch-cooking-beginners

BetterHelp Editorial Team. (2024, March 2). *What can you do if you live in fear of being judged? | BetterHelp.* https://www.betterhelp.com/advice/general/what-can-you-do-if-you-live-in-fear-of-being-judged/

BetterHelp Editorial Team. (2024b, March 11). *Six family types and their unique dynamics | BetterHelp.* https://www.betterhelp.com/advice/family/there-are-6-different-family-types-and-each-one-has-a-unique-family-dynamic/

Boogaard, K. (2024, February 6). *How to write SMART goals (with examples).* Work Life by Atlassian. https://www.atlassian.com/blog/productivity/how-to-write-smart-goals#:~:text=What%20are%20SMART%20goals%3F,within%20a%20certain%20time%20frame.

Bullying Resources | Text HOME to 741741 for free support. (2024, May 7). Crisis Text Line. https://www.crisistextline.org/topics/bullying/#what-is-bullying-1

REFERENCES

Burgess, E. W., & Locke, H. J. (1945). *The family: from institution to companionship.* American Book Co.

Byju's Future School. (n.d.). *The psychology behind sibling rivalry (and how to imrpove it).* byjusfutureschool.com. Retrieved April 1, 2024, from https://www.byjusfutureschool.com/blog/the-psychology-behind-sibling-conflict/#:~:text=Researchers%20also%20believe%20that%20sibling,or%20unique%20from%20their%20siblings.

Cargioli, P. (2023, August 16). *How to forgive a friend who hurt you + Affirmations.* Open Heart Holistic Therapy. https://openheartholistictherapy.com/blog/how-to-forgive-a-friend-who-hurt-you-affirmations

CDC - Scabies - General Information - Frequently asked questions (FAQs). (n.d.). https://www.cdc.gov/parasites/scabies/gen_info/faqs.html#:~:text=I%20treat%20myself%3F-,What%20is%20scabies%3F,a%20pimple%2Dlike%20skin%20rash.

Chen, H., et al. (2020, August 18). *Career Adaptability Research: A literature review with scientific knowledge mapping in Web of Science.* National Library of Medicine. https://www.ncbi.nlm.nih.gov/pmc/articles/PMC7459956/

ChristineXP. (2024, January 25). *10 Things Every Teen Should Know About Dealing with a Mental Health Issue.* Discovery Mood & Anxiety Program. https://discoverymood.com/blog/10-tips-teen-dealing-with-a-mental-health/

Cleveland Clinic. (2023, April 22). *FOMO is real: How the fear of missing out affects your health.* https://health.clevelandclinic.org/understanding-fomo

Coursera Staff. (2024b, March 27). *8 types of coding jobs (+ tips to get hired)*. Coursera. https://www.coursera.org/articles/coding-jobs

Deeper Signals. (n.d.). *Deeper Signals | The Top 5 Reasons Why Feedback is Critical to Success*. https://www.deepersignals.com/blog/the-top-5-reasons-why-feedback-is-critical-to-success

DeNicola, L. (2023, March 10). *How to manage your privacy settings on social media*. https://www.experian.com/blogs/ask-experian/how-to-manage-your-privacy-settings-on-social-media/

Dhaliwal, J. (2024, May 8). *How to spot fake news in your social media feed*. McAfee Blog. https://www.mcafee.com/blogs/internet-security/spot-fake-news-and-misinformation-in-your-social-media-feed/

Digital boundaries - love is respect. (2023, March 24). Love Is Respect. https://www.loveisrespect.org/resources/digital-boundaries/

Digital Detox: How to limit screen time for kids. (n.d.). CHOA | Strong4Life. https://www.strong4life.com/en/parenting/screen-time/digital-detox-how-to-limit-screen-time-for-kids

Dorwart, L. (2023, November 8). *Where are your Pressure Points—And how can you use them?* Health. https://www.health.com/pressure-points-7973884#:~:text=Pressure%20points%20are%20specific%20points,medicine%2C%20reflexology%2C%20and%20acupressure.

Dratch, D. (2024, February 23). *7 tactics car salespeople hope you don't know (and how to beat them)*. Bankrate. https://www.bankrate.com/loans/auto-loans/how-to-deal-with-car-salesmen/#prepare

Epstein, L. (2022, December 17). *Advantages and Disadvantages of using coupons for your business*. Investopedia. https://www.investopedia.com/articles/personal-finance/051815/pros-cons-using-coupons-your-business.asp#:~:text=Coupons%20can%20be%20used%20to,to%20buy%20from%20your%20store.

Evaluating web sources. (n.d.). Harvard Guide to Using Sources. https://usingsources.fas.harvard.edu/evaluating-web-sources-0

Family roles |. (n.d.). https://innerchange.com/parents-resources/family-roles/

Fantin, E. (2024, February 5). *17 handy educational apps for teens! - Your Teen Magazine*. Your Teen Magazine. https://yourteenmag.com/technology/educational-apps-for-teens

Ferguson, S. (2023, April 18). *What is breathwork meditation?* Healthline. https://www.healthline.com/health/breath-work-meditation#benefits

Fontinelle, A. (2022, September 22). *Why do companies print coupons?* Investopedia. https://www.investopedia.com/financial-edge/0911/why-do-companies-print-coupons.aspx#:~:text=Manufacturers%20and%20stores%20benefit%20from,a%20specific%20company%20or%20product.

Gavin, M. (2022, February). *Why exercise is wise*. Nemours TeensHealth. https://kidshealth.org/en/teens/exercise-wise.html

Global, B. (2023, June 20). *The Dos and Don'ts of Networking: Etiquette Tips for Success*. BNI. https://www.bni.com/the-latest/blog-news/the-dos-and-donts-of-networking-etiquette-tips-for-success

GOBankingRates. (n.d.). 5 of the Most Promising Industries To Invest In for 2024. *Nasdaq*. https://www.nasdaq.com/articles/5-of-the-most-promising-industries-to-invest-in-for-2024

Grocery Shopping | MyPlate. (n.d.). https://www.myplate.gov/tip-sheet/grocery-shopping

Gupta, S. (2023, May 26). *The Importance of Self-Reflection: How looking inward can improve your Mental health*. Verywell Mind. https://www.verywellmind.com/self-reflection-importance-benefits-and-strategies-7500858#toc-why-is-self-reflection-so-important

Hall, T. (2023, September 11). *12 At-Home workout Ideas for Teenagers*. ASFA. https://www.americansportandfitness.com/blogs/fitness-blog/12-at-home-workout-ideas-for-teenagers

Healthdirect Australia. (2023, October 31). *Personal hygiene*. Healthdirect. https://www.healthdirect.gov.au/personal-hygiene

Healthdirect Australia. (n.d.). *Threadworms (pinworms)*. Symptoms and Treatment | Healthdirect. https://www.healthdirect.gov.au/threadworms-pinworms

Horton, H. (2024, April 23). *The Ultimate Guide to coding for Teens*. TeacherVision. https://www.teachervision.com/educational-technology/top-5-free-coding-tools-for-teens

How can I develop a support network? | DO-IT. (n.d.). https://www.washington.edu/doit/how-can-i-develop-support-network#:~:text=A%20support%20network%20refers%20to,members%2C%20friends%2C%20and%20teachers.

How is Life Tree(ting) You?: Trust, Safety, and Respect - The Importance of Boundaries. (n.d.). Student Affairs.

REFERENCES

https://studentaffairs.stanford.edu/how-life-treeting-you-importance-of-boundaries#:~:text=Boundaries%20help%20determine%20what%20is,safety%2C%20and%20respect%20in%20relationships.

How to identify and manage your emotional triggers. (2020, November 13). Healthline. https://www.healthline.com/health/mental-health/emotional-triggers

How to Meditate. (n.d.). Mindful.org. https://www.mindful.org/how-to-meditate/#basics

How to secure your home Wi-Fi network. (2024, April 23). Consumer Advice. https://consumer.ftc.gov/articles/how-secure-your-home-wi-fi-network#:~:text=Encryption%20scrambles%20the%20information%20sent,WPA3%20Personal%20or%20WPA2%20Personal.

Ilett, S. (2019, September 27). *What is SPF (Sun Protection Factor)*. Reef Repair. https://www.reefrepair.com/education/science/what-is-spf-sun-protection-factor/

Indeed Editorial Team. (2023, January 31). *Workplace Skills: Definition and Examples*. Indeed. https://www.indeed.com/career-advice/career-development/workplace-skills

Indeed Editorial Team. (2023, March 29). *10 tips to Help you Build a Network (With Benefits)*. https://www.indeed.com/career-advice/career-development/build-a-network

Industries Expected to Thrive in 2024. (2023, November 28). PNC. https://www.pnc.com/insights/small-business/growing-your-business/industries-expected-to-thrive-in-2024.html

Jalali, R. (2022, December 7). How technology is being used for social good. *Forbes.* https://www.forbes.com/sites/forbestechcouncil/2022/12/06/how-technology-is-being-used-for-social-good/?sh=3f755c351b12

Jpotyraj. (2022, January 28). *How to Protect Your Child or Teen from Identity Theft: Cybersecurity Best Practices - UT Austin Boot Camps.* UT Austin Boot Camps. https://techbootcamps.utexas.edu/blog/how-to-protect-your-child-or-teen-from-identity-theft-cybersecurity-best-practices/

Journey. (n.d.). *Journey.Cloud - free online journal & diary.* Journey.Cloud. https://journey.cloud/reflective-journal

Koifman, N. (2023, July 6). The importance of mentorship. *Forbes.* https://www.forbes.com/sites/forbesbusinesscouncil/2023/07/05/the-importance-of-mentorship/?sh=4e1ffc73693d

Kristenson, S. (2023, December 9). *60 positive affirmations for those moments of self doubt.* Happier Human. https://www.happierhuman.com/affirmations-self-doubt/

Lohmann, R. (2010, December 11). *Cyber etiquette for teens.* Psychology Today. https://www.psychologytoday.com/us/blog/teen-angst/201012/cyber-etiquette-teens

Lunch, W. (2024, March 12). *Meal planning for beginners (Meal Plan template inside!).* Workweek Lunch. https://workweeklunch.com/meal-planning-for-beginners/

May, L. (2022, May 26). *Twenty kitchen skills every teen needs to know before they leave for University — The Organic Cookery School.* The Organic Cookery School. https://www.organiccookeryschool.org/blog//20-kitchen-skills-every-teen-needs-to-know-before-they-leave-for-uni

Mayer, C. (2021, December 6). *Sibling Dynamics: What is Fair? — Growing Minds Psychology*. Growing Minds Psychology. https://www.growingmindsnyc.com/blog/sibling-dynamics-what-is-fair

McCartney, A. (2023, November 8). What is coding and what is it used for? | ComputerScience.org. *ComputerScience.org*. https://www.computerscience.org/resources/what-is-coding-used-for/

McRae, A. (2023, November 27). *How to break down big Goals | The Ultimate Guide*. Ana McRae Coaching. https://anamcrae.ca/how-to-break-down-your-goals/

Melissa. (2022, October 24). *10 best study space tips*. Joyce. https://www.joyce.edu/blog/10-best-study-space-tips/

Miller, M. (2022, March 14). *The 3 parts of empathy: thoughts, feelings and actions*. Six Seconds. https://www.6seconds.org/2022/03/14/3-parts-of-empathy/

MSEd, K. C. (2022, October 13). *Social comparison Theory in Psychology*. Verywell Mind. https://www.verywellmind.com/what-is-the-social-comparison-process-2795872#:~:text=The%20social%20comparison%20process%20involves,with%20whom%20we%20are%20similar.

MSEd, K. C. (2023, November 9). *How to improve your Self-Control*. Verywell Mind. https://www.verywellmind.com/psychology-of-self-control-4177125#:~:text=You%20can%20improve%20your%20own,regulate%20your%20behavior%20more%20effectively.

M, T. (2023, April 12). *How to leverage social media to enhance your professional network and job search*. https://www.linkedin.com/pulse/how-leverage-social-media-enhance-your-professional-job-marler-mba/

National Cybersecurity Alliance. (2024, March 25). *Manage your privacy settings*.
https://staysafeonline.org/resources/manage-your-privacy-settings/

Newport Academy. (2024, January 9). *How to Help Teens Unplug*.
https://www.newportacademy.com/resources/restoring-families/digital-detox/

Next Insurance. (2023, December 1). *12 Fastest growing small businesses of 2024 | NEXT*.
https://www.nextinsurance.com/blog/fastest-growing-small-businesses/

Normal Emotions: Understanding the Spectrum of Human Feelings : Live Well Psychiatry : Psychiatrists. (n.d.).
https://www.livewellpsychiatry.com/blog/normal-emotions-understanding-the-spectrum-of-human-feelings

Nutrition for Teens. (n.d.).
https://www.johnmuirhealth.com/health-education/health-wellness/childrens-health/nutrition-teens.html#:~:text=The%20best%20way%20your%20teen,the%20right%20balance%20of%20nutrients.

Odukoya, A. (2023, October 30). *The changing generational values*. Imagine | Johns Hopkins University.
https://imagine.jhu.edu/blog/2022/11/17/the-changing-generational-values/

Office, C. (2020, July 29). *Developing healthy coping skills for resilience*. Human Resources | Washington University in St. Louis. https://hr.wustl.edu/developing-healthy-coping-skills-for-resilience/

Okoye, A. (2024, January 19). *How screen time affects teens' sleep*. Sleep Doctor. https://sleepdoctor.com/teens/how-screen-time-affects-teens-

REFERENCES

sleep/#:~:text=Teens%20who%20spend%20a%20lot,experience%20tiredness%20during%20the%20day.

Oxford Languages and Google - English | Oxford Languages. (2024, January 16). https://languages.oup.com/google-dictionary-en/

Patient rights and responsibilities. (n.d.). Wisconsin Department of Employee Trust Funds. https://etf.wi.gov/health-benefits/patient-rights-and-responsibilities#:~:text=You%20have%20the%20following%20rights,presented%20in%20an%20understandable%20manner.

Perspective taking | College of Biological Sciences. (n.d.). https://cbs.umn.edu/student-services/student-engagement/competency-areas/perspective-taking#:~:text=Considering%20perspectives%20other%20than%20one's,understanding%2C%20and%20appreciation%20of%20others.

Pressure points for stress relief. (2023, August 7). https://www.hackensackmeridianhealth.org/en/healthu/2023/08/07/pressure-points-for-stress-relief

Professional, C. C. M. (n.d.). *Body odor*. Cleveland Clinic. https://my.clevelandclinic.org/health/symptoms/17865-body-odor

Psychology Today Staff. (n.d.). *Empathy*. psychologytoday.com. Retrieved March 19, 2024, from https://www.psychologytoday.com/us/basics/empathy

Reading food labels. (2022, March). Neumors KidsHealth. https://kidshealth.org/en/parents/food-labels.html

Rd, J. K. M. (2020, August 24). *40 Healthy snacks for hungry Teens*. Healthline. https://www.healthline.com/nutrition/snacks-for-teens#high-protein

Reid, D. (2022, September 27). *Why diversity is really our greatest strength*. Psychology Today. https://www.psychologytoday.com/us/blog/coaching-corner/202209/why-diversity-is-really-our-greatest-strength

Resilience is Underpinned by Optimism. (n.d.). https://www.centreforoptimism.com/resilience

Reskilling Revolution: Preparing 1 billion people for tomorrow's economy. (2024, January 16). World Economic Forum. https://www.weforum.org/impact/reskilling-revolution-reaching-600-million-people-by-2030/

Review-Vise. (2023, September 14). *Future-Proof Your Career: Top 10 online skills for future*. https://www.linkedin.com/pulse/future-proof-your-career-top-10-online-skills-future-alex-archives/

Risks of oversharing on social media. (n.d.). New York Tech Blogs. https://blogs.nyit.edu/the_cyber_corner/risks_of_oversharing_on_social_media#:~:text=Personal%20Data%20Exposure%3A%20When%20you,you%20or%20launch%20targeted%20attacks.

Routley, N. (2021, April 9). *A visual guide to human emotion*. Visual Capitalist. https://www.visualcapitalist.com/a-visual-guide-to-human-emotion/#google_vignette

Sanders, L. (2023, May 8). *Trust in Media 2023: What news outlets do Americans trust most for information?* YouGov. https://today.yougov.com/politics/articles/45671-trust-in-media-2023-what-news-outlets-trust-poll

Screen time in teenagers: how can we manage it? | My Kids Vision. (n.d.). https://www.mykidsvision.org/knowledge-centre/screen-time-in-teenagers-how-can-we-manage-it#how-much-screen-time-should-i-aim-for-with-my-teenager?

Self-Doubt: Definition, causes, & how to overcome it. (n.d.). The Berkeley Well-Being Institute. https://www.berkeleywellbeing.com/self-doubt.html

self-reflection. (2024). https://dictionary.cambridge.org/us/dictionary/english/self-reflection

Seligman, M. E. (2021, September 17). *Building resilience*. Harvard Business Review. https://hbr.org/2011/04/building-resilience

Smith, M., MA. (2024, February 28). *Sleep Disorders and Problems: Types, causes, treatment*. HelpGuide.org. https://www.helpguide.org/articles/sleep/sleep-disorders-and-problems.htm

Staff, C. (2024, February 2). *Strategies in Communication: Your guide to Better connections*. Coursera. https://www.coursera.org/articles/strategies-in-communication

Stress. (2022, June 17). https://www.who.int/news-room/questions-and-answers/item/stress#:~:text=Stress%20can%20be%20defined%20as,experiences%20stress%20to%20some%20degree.

Stress management: How to tell the difference between good and bad stress. (2021, January 18). Summa Health. https://www.summahealth.org/flourish/entries/2021/01/stress-management-how-to-tell-the-difference-between-good-and-bad-stress#:~:text=Good%20stress%2C%20or%20eustress%2C%20is,is%20no%20threat%20or%20fear.

Sun, A. (2022, January 17). *Why Quality Over Price is Always the Sustainable Choice?* https://www.linkedin.com/pulse/why-quality-over-price-always-sustainable-choice-amy-sun/

Svitorka, T. (2024, February 9). Master Small Talk: 6 tips for Better Conversations and Less awkwardness. *Tomas Svitorka - London Life Coach*. https://tomassvitorka.com/master-small-talk/

Thensf. (2020, November 10). *How to Make a Sleep-Friendly Bedroom - National Sleep Foundation*. National Sleep Foundation. https://www.thensf.org/how-to-make-a-sleep-friendly-bedroom/

The Skin Cancer Foundation. (2023, May 23). *Ask the Expert: Does a High SPF Protect My Skin Better?* https://www.skincancer.org/blog/ask-the-expert-does-a-high-spf-protect-my-skin-better/#:~:text=What%20Does%20the%20SPF%20Number,you%20weren't%20wearing%20sunscreen.

The Pomodoro technique — why it works & how to do it. (n.d.). Todoist. https://todoist.com/productivity-methods/pomodoro-technique

The value of building a Social Media Community - Digital Marketing Lesson - DMI. (n.d.). Digital Marketing Institute. https://digitalmarketinginstitute.com/resources/lessons/social-media-marketing_the-value-of-building-a-social-media-community_ehof

Time Management for Teens: care instructions. (n.d.). https://myhealth.alberta.ca/Health/aftercareinformation/pages/conditions.aspx?hwid=ug6046

Tipalti. (2023, October 24). Best Wellness Apps in 2023 | Tipalti. *Tipalti*. https://tipalti.com/guide/best-wellness-apps-2023/

Tips and strategies to manage Anxiety and stress | Anxiety and Depression Association of America, ADAA. (n.d.). https://adaa.org/tips

Too much time on screens? Screen time effects and guidelines for children and young people. (n.d.). Australian Institute of

Family Studies. https://aifs.gov.au/resources/short-articles/too-much-time-screens#:~:text=For%20screen%20time%2C%20the%20guidelines,years%20(not%20including%20schoolwork).

Trek, S. (2021, May 10). *5 home maintenance skills Every teen should learn - Skill Trek*. Skill Trek. https://skilltrekker.com/5-home-maintenance-skills-for-teens/

Tricaso, K. (2023, January 25). *What is a Chosen Family & How to Build Your Own*. Modern Intimacy. https://www.modernintimacy.com/what-is-a-chosen-family-how-to-build-your-own/

Ultimate Guide: Copper's Guide to Budgeting (for teens). (n.d.). https://www.getcopper.com/guide/budgeting#faqs

Van Schaik, J. (2018, August 15). The 7 Pillars Of True Friendship - Joren van Schaik - Medium. *Medium*. https://jorenvanschaik.medium.com/the-7-pillars-of-true-friendship-f1d30f37b06a

Vision Boards: What are they & How to create one in 5 steps. (n.d.). https://www.betterup.com/blog/how-to-create-vision-board

Vogels, E. (2022, December 15). *Teens and Cyberbullying 2022*. Pew Research Center. https://www.pewresearch.org/internet/2022/12/15/teens-and-cyberbullying-2022/

Vogel, L. (2019, June 24). *Quality of kids' screen time matters as much as quantity*. https://www.ncbi.nlm.nih.gov/pmc/articles/PMC6592813/

Walden University. (2023, February 15). Cybersecurity 101: Why choosing a secure password is so important. *Walden University*. https://www.waldenu.edu/programs/information-technology/resource/cybersecurity-101-why-choosing-a-secure-password-in-so-important#:~:text=Strong%20passwords%20are%20of%20the,from%20cyber%20threats%20and%20hackers.

Warning signs of mental illness. (n.d.).
https://www.psychiatry.org/patients-families/warning-signs-of-mental-illness

Ways to incorporate movement into your everyday life. (n.d.). Memorial Hermann. Retrieved May 15, 2024, from https://www.memorialhermann.org/health-wellness/fitness/incorporate-movement-into-everyday-life

WebMD Editorial Contributors. (2023a, January 18). *Depression vs. Anxiety: Which One Do I Have?* WebMD. https://www.webmd.com/depression/depression-or-anxiety

Wendt, T. (2022, November 1). *Why family traditions matter.* WebMD. https://www.webmd.com/balance/why-family-traditions-matter

What is Creative Coding? (n.d.). Meadows School of the Arts, SMU. https://www.smu.edu/meadows/newsandevents/news/2023/what-is-creative-coding#:~:text=Creative%20coding%20is%20the%20practice,efficiency%20in%20a%20digital%20space.

What is Emotional Expression? (n.d.). https://www.kansashealthsystem.com/health-resources/turning-point/programs/resilience-toolbox/emotional-expression/what-is-emotional-expression

World Health Organization: WHO. (2022, June 8). *Mental disorders.* https://www.who.int/news-room/fact-sheets/detail/mental-disorders

Why Extracurricular Activities and Sports Are So Important - St. Johnsbury Academy. (n.d.). St. Johnsbury Academy. https://stjacademy.org/a-culture-of-caring-and-respect/the-boarding-experience/7-things-in-common-with-the-best-private-schools/why-extracurricular/

Why is sleep important? | NHLBI, NIH. (2022, March 24). NHLBI, NIH. https://www.nhlbi.nih.gov/health/sleep/why-sleep-important#:~:text=During%20sleep%2C%20your%20body%20is,long%2Dterm)%20health%20problems.

Your personal brand - the heroic journey of teenagers. (2020, April 21). The Heroic Journey of Teenagers. https://teenheroicjourney.org/book/3-core-challenges/forming-an-identity/identity-picture/your-personal-brand/

Made in United States
Cleveland, OH
19 November 2024